Henry James' Travel

Henry James' Travel: Fiction and Non-Fiction offers a multifaceted approach to Henry James' idea and practice of travel from the perspective of the globalized world today. Each chapter addresses a different selection of James' fiction and non-fiction and offers a different approach towards the ideas that are still with us today: history reflected in art and architecture, the tourist gaze, museum culture, transnationalism, and the return home. As a whole, the book encompasses both early and late fiction and non-fiction by Henry James, giving the reader a sense of how his idea of travel evolved over several decades of his creative activity and shows how thin the line between fiction and non-fiction travel writing really is.

Mirosława Buchholtz is Professor of English and Head of the English Department at Nicolaus Copernicus University, Poland. She has published academic books, including a monograph on Henry James. She is former President of the Henry James Society.

Henry James' Travel

Fiction and Non-Fiction

Edited by Mirosława Buchholtz

Routledge
Taylor & Francis Group

LONDON AND NEW YORK

First published 2019
by Routledge
4 Park Square, Milton Park, Abingdon, Oxon OX14 4RN

and by Routledge
605 Third Avenue, New York, NY 10017

First issued in paperback 2023

Routledge is an imprint of the Taylor & Francis Group, an informa business

© 2019 selection and editorial matter, Mirosława Buchholtz; individual chapters, the contributors

Publisher's Note
The publisher has gone to great lengths to ensure the quality of this reprint but points out that some imperfections in the original copies may be apparent.

British Library Cataloguing-in-Publication Data
A catalogue record for this book is available from the British Library

Library of Congress Cataloging-in-Publication Data
Names: Buchholtz, Mirosława, editor.
Title: Henry James' travel : fiction and non-fiction / edited by Mirosława Buchholtz.
Description: Abingdon, Oxon ; New York, NY : Routledge, 2019. | Includes bibliographical references and index.
Identifiers: LCCN 2018038784 | ISBN 9781138350526 (hardback : alk. paper) | ISBN 9780429789083 (epub) | ISBN 9780429789090 (web pdf) | ISBN 9780429789076 (mobikindle)
Subjects: LCSH: James, Henry, 1843-1916—Criticism and interpretation. | James, Henry, 1843-1916—Travel. | Travelers' writings, American—History and criticism. | Travel in literature.
Classification: LCC PS2127.T74 H46 2019 | DDC 813/.4—dc23
LC record available at https://lccn.loc.gov/2018038784

ISBN 13: 978-1-032-65353-2 (pbk)
ISBN 13: 978-1-138-35052-6 (hbk)
ISBN 13: 978-0-429-43580-5 (ebk)

DOI: 10.4324/9780429435805

Typeset in Times New Roman
by Apex CoVantage, LLC

Contents

Figures

Contributors

Geoff Bender is Assistant Professor of English at the State University of New York College at Cortland, where he teaches courses in American and world literature, film, and English education. His recent essays can be found in such journals as *The Hawthorne Review* and *Image & Text*, and his recent poetry in *Kestrel*, *The Chiron Review*, and elsewhere. His monograph *Casting the Great Original: Class, Classicism, and the Bourgeois Fear of Modernity*, which explores the politics of classicism in the American nineteenth century, is, at long last, near completion.

Mirosława Buchholtz is Professor of English and Director of the English Department at Nicolaus Copernicus University in Toruń, Poland, where she teaches American and Canadian literature, film adaptations of literature and biography, life writing, and postcolonial studies. A graduate of the Jagiellonian University (Poland) and Brandeis University (USA), she has published some seventy articles, six books (including *Henry James and the Art of Auto/biography* in 2014), sixteen edited volumes (for example, *The Visual and the Verbal in Film, Drama, Literature and Biography* in 2012 and *Henry James Goes to War* in 2014), four edited issues of academic journals (including *Henry James: The Writer's Museum* for *Litteraria Copernicana* in 2017), and numerous reviews and translations. She is former President of the Henry James Society (2017) and a member of the Polish Accreditation Committee (quality assurance agency), since 2012.

Urszula Gołębiowska, a graduate of the University of Wrocław and Maria Curie-Skłodowska University in Lublin, is Assistant Professor at the Institute of Modern Languages, University of Zielona Góra, Poland, where she teaches American literature, introduction to literary studies, intertextuality, and adaptation. She has published articles on the fiction of Henry James, Alice Munro, J. M. Coetzee, and Paul Bowles. She has recently completed a book entitled *The Lesson of the Master. Alterity and Subjectivity in Henry James's Fiction*, which is due to appear in 2019.

Allen Hibbard is Professor of English and Director of the Middle East Center at Middle Tennessee State University. He received his B.A. in International Studies from the American University in Washington, DC, and his Ph.D. in English from the University of Washington in Seattle. From 1985 to 1989 he taught at the American University in Cairo and from 1992 to 1994 he was a Fulbright lecturer (in American literature) at Damascus University. His research and teaching interests include modernism, postmodernism, literary theory, the novel, translation, and transnational movement, with a focus on interactions between the United States and the Arab world. Hibbard has written two books on Paul Bowles (*Paul Bowles: A Study of the Short Fiction*, 1993, and *Paul Bowles, Magic & Morocco*, 2004), edited *Conversations with William S Burroughs* (2000), and published a collection of his own stories in Arabic (Damascus, 1994). He has contributed essays to more than a dozen edited volumes. His essays, stories, translations, and reviews have appeared in *American Literature*, *Centennial Review*, *Cimarron Review*, *Comparative Literature Studies*, *Grand Street*, *International Literary Quarterly*, *Interventions*, *Jadiliyya*, *Middle East Studies Bulletin*, *Passport*, and elsewhere. With his colleague Osama Esber, he is currently completing a translation of *A Banquet for Seaweed*, a novel by contemporary Syrian writer Haidar.

Ágnes Zsófia Kovács is Associate Professor at the Department of American Studies, University of Szeged, Hungary. Her areas of academic interest and teaching include late nineteenth-century, early twentieth-century, and contemporary American fiction, with a special interest in Henry James's fictitious and non-fiction representations of the moral imagination. Her current research into travel writing involves re-mapping travel texts by Edith Wharton, for which she received a Beinecke Fellowship in 2017. Her other (prospective) research interest is in multicultural American identity prose, more specifically in Toni Morrison's practice of literary memory as moral imagination. Ágnes Zsófia Kovács has published two books: *The Function of the Imagination in the Writings of Henry James* (2006) and *Literature in Context* (2010) and has co-edited *Space, Gender and the Gaze* (2017).

Selma Mokrani is Maître de Conférences (Associate Professor) at the Department of English at Badji-Mokhtar-Annaba University in Annaba, Algeria, where she teaches English literature, literary criticism and theory, research design and methodology, and literary pragmatics. Her doctoral thesis is about nation, race, empire, and travel in the works of Henry James, George Eliot, Edith Wharton, and E. M. Forster. She has published articles on the national symbolic ("Henry James's America: 'The Historic Desert' in Quest of 'The Historic Mausoleum'" in 2011 and " 'The Gift of the Stranger': Elkader as a Cultural Utopia" in 2016); on the role of travel writing in the construction of a disjunctive empire (for example, "Beyond the Frame: Fez in Edith Wharton's *In Morocco* and Pierre Loti's *Au Maroc*," and "Edith Wharton's Maghreb: Identity Politics and Dis/Conjunctive Encounters," in 2011); and on the ambivalent writing of empire ("E. M. Forster and the Writing of Empire: Aestheticentrism, Humanism, and Liberal Guilt" in 2010). Amongst her major present research interests are the complex intersections of spatial studies, postcolonial studies, and travel writing.

Hitomi Nabae is Professor of American Literature and Comparative Literature at Kobe City University of Foreign Studies, Kobe, Japan. She earned her B.A. and M.A. at Kobe College (Japan) and completed her doctorate courses at Kwansei Gakuin University (Japan). She received her Ph.D. from Stanford University (USA) in 2000. She has published *The Spirit of No Place: Reportage, Translation and Re-told Stories in Lafcadio Hearn* (Kobe City University of Foreign Studies, 2014), co-translated with Keiko Beppu *Dear Munificent Friends: James's Letters to Four Women* by Susan Gunter (Osaka Kyoiku-Tosho, 2016), and co-edited with Satomi Shigemi and Yoshio Nakamura a collection of essays, *Henry James, Now: Commemorating the 100th Year of His Death* (Eihosha, 2016). She is interested in modernity, expatriatism, art, and ghosts, and has written on Henry James, Edith Wharton, Mina Loy, and Lafcadio Hearn.

Abbreviations

Introduction[1]

Mirosława Buchholtz

The world has grown smaller since Henry James's time. Today tourists visit regularly and with little effort places where he had never ventured, or even imagined as viable destinations. He envisaged the possibility of his characters travelling to Japan (for example, Isabel Archer in *The Portrait of a Lady*) and coming home from the British colonies (the case of General Fancourt in "The Lesson of the Master"), but in his own travels he stayed on well-trodden paths of the usual Grand Tour in Europe. Would it be true, however, to say that he was a tourist rather than an explorer? It may well be an illusion after all to think that he went where everybody else was going and saw only what everybody else was taking in, seeking pleasure and delight, and seeking to please and delight the readers of his travel accounts. His *Little Tour in France*, for example, bears witness to his going against the grain and subverting popular beliefs, such as the then and now current claim that Paris is the essential France. In defiance of the idea of the Grand Tour, he boldly proposed a *Little* Tour of the provinces, and of the past that is alive in small or relatively small places and objects. Although apparently quite conventional, he was a special kind of tourist. His visit to the United States after the Odyssean absence of over twenty years is another proof of that. His culture shock written into *The American Scene* is all the more astounding as in 1904 James was to all appearances going home. The account of his American travel is in addition an unfinished larger project. While in the United States and lecturing mostly on Balzac, he travelled not only southward, which is the direction *The American Scene* takes, but also westward.[2] Whatever notes may exist of that latter part of his travels, they were never gathered in the projected second volume.

Henry James was, as Hendrik Hertzberg puts it, "almost literally, a born traveler" (2016: viii). His first crossing of the Atlantic aboard a luxury steamship the *Great Western* occurred when he was six months old in October 1843. The future novelist's father and namesake could afford it; he had come (not without litigation though) into his share of his own father's estate – "reputedly the second largest private fortune in New York State" (Kaplan 1992: 7). The family stayed in England and France until 1845. The four more crossings in Henry James's teens, to which Hertzberg refers (2016: ix), were due to his father's restlessness, disguised as the search for "a better sensuous education" for his progeny (qtd. in Anesko 2016: xvii). This time the family tours also included Switzerland and Germany. After a prolonged stay in the United States in the 1860s, in 1869 Henry James Jr. set out for Europe again, this time on his own. He was not as adventurous as his "ideal elder brother" William, who in 1865 joined a scientific expedition to the Amazon, but he was venturesome in his own way, too; not only was he travelling by himself, but he also expanded the perimeters of his explorations to include Italy. Those discoveries made an indelible impression that shines through his subsequent fiction, *Roderick Hudson* and "The Madonna of the Future," to name just two examples.

In the summer and autumn of 1872 James chaperoned his sister Alice and his aunt Kate on their tour of England, France, Switzerland, Italy, Austria, and Germany (Anesko 2016: xviii), but the idea of settling down in Europe was already gestating. His first choice (and stop) was Paris, where he worked as a correspondent for the *New-York Tribune*, but in December 1876 he moved to London, which became his home for subsequent years. Trips to "the Continent," especially France and Italy, became a pattern throughout his creative life. Some of his fiction and non-fiction was written during such travels and prolonged stays abroad. Were those indeed foreign parts for James, or perhaps much rather the many different homes that his imagination inhabited? The busy social life in London three or four years into his expatriation may also count as an ethnographic venture. The reservedly gleeful report about "din[ing] out during the past winter 107 times!" in a letter to Grace Norton of 8 June 1879 (James *CL78–80* 2014: 203) reflects his sense of transcultural success in the adoptive homeland.

His visit to the United States for a period of several months in 1881–1882 began as a triumphant return of a successful author to the place of his birth. He was lionized in New York, but the joy was tempered by illness and death in the family; on his return Henry James saw his ailing brother Wilky for the first time in ten years and by the end of January 1882 he mourned his mother's death. His next visit to the United States at the turn of 1882 and 1883 was prompted by the failing health of his father, who died in December 1882. Wilky died within a year, in November 1883. When Henry James's sister Alice arrived in England in 1884, it seemed that she only came for a visit, but her nervous ailment prevented travel, and she decided to stay near her favourite brother. There were now two of them living as expatriates in England until Alice's death in 1892.

Another kind of "expatriation" (or rather part-time rustication) from urban to rural surroundings occurred in 1898, following James's decision to rent Lamb House in Rye, Sussex (Figure 0.1).[3] This is where Henry James returned *home* from the lecture tour of the United States in 1904–1905 and stayed on and off until 1912, when he took again an apartment in London. Saying goodbye to people and places became a ritual in the first decade of the twentieth century. So, for example, he paid his last respects to Rome in 1907. He knew he would never return, and never did. The Eternal City would live on, but James was increasingly aware of his own mortality, and imagined in the evocative late essay "Is There a Life after Death?" (1910) the last journey of consciousness. The travels in 1910 were for the sake of health and to funerals. He first visited a German spa with ailing William and then travelled with him to the United States (Moore 1974: 118). Henry James's younger brother Robertson died in June and his elder brother William in August 1910. Henry James's posthumous crossing of the Atlantic occurred during the Great War. When he died in 1916, his sister-in-law Alice James smuggled his ashes to bury them at the family plot in Cambridge, Massachusetts (Gunter 2009: 304).

Figure 0.1 Lamb House in Rye. Digital photograph by Sonoko Saito, 2016. The white plaque far right reads: "HENRY JAMES/AUTHOR/LIVED HERE/1898–1916."

As a young author James benefitted from the flourishing magazine market and his early travel writing catered for the newly acquired needs of cultured middle and upper-middle class of American readers. Their desire to discover places was immense, there financial means less so, and the young author fulfilled gladly the role of a surrogate tourist. He did not invent travel writing as a genre, but as a reader of accounts by Stendhal, Bayard Taylor, Orville Dewey, John Ruskin, and no doubt many others, as Ágnes Kovács, Geoff Bender, and Selma Mokrani show on the following pages, he took stock of both the places he visited and the traditions of representing them in fiction and non-fiction. In this volume we use the double focus and show how the experience of travel informs not only James's travelogues, but also his tales and novels.

When *A Little Tour in France* came out in Boston in 1884,[4] James's travel writing still seemed to be his main asset, as the list of his "latest works" on the counter-title page indicates (Figure 0.2). With the exception of "Daisy Miller," which is in itself, as Roslyn Jolly put it, "a story about, and for, tourists" (2010: 346), each of the listed titles contains a spatial reference:

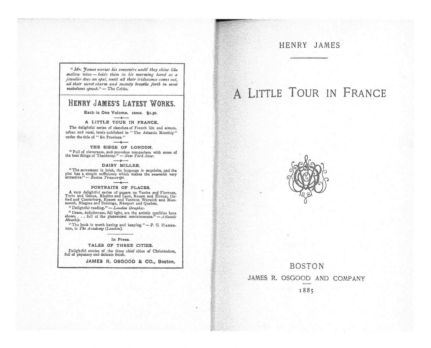

Figure 0.2 The title and counter-title pages of *A Little Tour in France*. Scanned by Mirosława Buchholtz.

to France, London, or else "places" and "cities." Apart from the titles mentioned in the advertisement, James's travel books include also *Transatlantic Sketches* (1875), *English Hours* (1905), *The American Scene* (1907), and *Italian Hours* (1909). The sheer time span of the publications testifies to the significance of travel in the novelist's career. The two volumes of James's *Collected Travel Writing* published by the Library of America in 1993 contain, apart from his major travel writings, miscellanea gathered under the heading of "Other Travels." To have a complete picture of James's travel accounts, however, one would also need to consider his letters. The ongoing effort of Greg W. Zacharias and his co-editors has opened up a whole new world of opportunities for scholars who can now see the many aspects of both James's travel and travel writing reflected in his correspondence: the glory of sightseeing (and thematization of "Cathedrals") in his letter to his sister Alice James (aged twenty) of 7 May 1869 (James *CL55–72* vol. 1 2006: 306), the justification of travel expenses as investment in "plain physical improvement" in his letter to Henry James Sr. of 10 May 1869 (James *CL55–72* vol. 1 2006: 310), and the balance sheet of magnificence and horror of travel in his letter to "Dearest mamman de mon coeur" of 19 May 1869 (James *CL55–72* vol. 2 2006: 5). These few examples from James's early correspondence mark only the beginning of vast opportunities for further discoveries.

So far within the past sixty years the significance of travel and expatriation for the novelist's work has been addressed in studies focused on his American, German, French, or cosmopolitan experience in books by Quentin Anderson, Evelyn A. Hovanec, Pierre A. Walker, Peter Brooks, Angus Wrenn, or Adeline R. Tintner, respectively, to name only a few. Roslyn Jolly has discussed several important issues related to travel and tourism in James's fiction and non-fiction, most notably the novelist's ironic anti-tourism, the phenomenon of social transgression inscribed in modern travel, or the investment of public spaces with unexpected new meanings. In a comparative reading of "Daisy Miller" and *The Wings of the Dove*, Jolly shows, for example, how a public setting turns into a quasi-private space (2010: 348, 351), and exposes tensions between possession and dispossession, or hotels and settlements in James's fiction. The opportunities to explore James's habits as a traveller and a travel(ling) writer seem endless, inviting research on "leisure spaces," such as hotels and ocean liners.[5]

The six authors of the following chapters come from four continents (North America, Europe, Africa, and Asia) and offer a multifaceted approach to Henry James's idea and practice of travel from the perspective of the globalized world today. Each chapter addresses a different selection of James's fiction and non-fiction and adopts a different approach towards the ideas that are part of our culture today: history reflected in art and architecture, ethnography, museums, transnationalism, tourist gaze, and return home. While it is a daunting task to address all of James's travel writings and all travels depicted in his fiction, our book offers spot analyses of specific issues that may inspire other scholars to apply the methodologies we offer to other fiction and non-fiction by James and to other writers to whom travel was a major part of their identity. As a whole, the book encompasses both early and late fiction and non-fiction by Henry James, giving the reader a sense of how his idea of travel evolved over several decades of his creative activity. Travel writing at the outset of his career may have been a stepping stone to fiction. "The Madonna of the Future" is an excellent example of this generic fluidity: it is both a detailed tour of Florence and a captivating narrative about artists and artisans in Italy, both Italians and Americans (at different stages of acculturation). Conversely, in his travel writings, James uses the fictional techniques of the persona and the juxtaposition of diverse characters (for example, a sentimental tourist vs. a modern fact-seeker, or the young traveller vs. the seasoned one).

James emerges as the epitome of literary cosmopolitism in Chapter 1, in which Allen Hibbard (USA) poses the question of how a comparative reading of *The Ambassadors* (1903) and *The American Scene* (1907) can deepen our understanding of transnational issues today, and vice versa. Attracted by the flair of Parisian lifestyle, James's protagonist, Lambert Strether, leaves behind the secure "old geography" of his American life, and has to reorient his perspective, realign his loyalties, and acquire a new more complex consciousness. Apart from identity and consciousness, Strether's situation provokes also questions of his financial status. The concept of "return," as a result of such considerations, takes on a double meaning in Hibbard's widening analysis not only of *The Ambassadors*, but also of "The Jolly Corner" (1908) and *The American Scene*. Looking further afield, Hibbard opens a wide perspective on post-Jamesian expatriate American novel and international studies of James's work.

In Chapter 2 Ágnes Zsófia Kovács (Hungary) presents James in his early forties as an insightful reader of material culture and cultural history in *A Little Tour in France* (1884, 1900). His reading is personal, as he claims, and inspired by the sights in rural France; rural meaning in this context outside of Paris. He takes the edge off his acute observations by calling himself a "sentimental" tourist, perhaps in the same vein as Lawrence Sterne. The span of his historical interest includes the Roman past, the Middle Ages, and the Renaissance. He unveils the different stages layer by layer, contributing to the then current debate of whether to restore ruins or not. There is a depth of historical reflection behind the ostensible delight in the picturesque, as Kovács so aptly shows in her chapter. She enriches the repertoire of methodologies by pointing not only to the picturesque but also to the architectural method in Henry James.

Travel was a cornerstone of Henry James's life, education, and literary work. Selma Mokrani (Algeria) traces in Chapter 3 James's repertoire of self-inventions and self-inscriptions in a succession of his travel writings in the several decades of his creative life, including texts revised and published again at the beginning of the new century: *A Little Tour in France* (1900) and *Italian Hours* (1909). The ethnographic impulse which prompted so much of his commissioned early travel writings evolves, as Mokrani cogently argues, into the autoethnography of *The American Scene*. In this chapter James stands in the limelight in his different capacities at first as a writer negotiating his own space within the tradition of travel writing, then as the master consolidating his authority, and finally as a desperate, vulnerable observer at the end of his journey home, to the past, and to the self. Mokrani offers yet another perspective on James as a self-reflexive travel writer and autobiographer in one.

Geoff Bender (USA) fills the scene in Chapter 4 with objects of art, models, artists, connoisseurs, and educators of tourists. The scene is shifting from the United States to Europe, alongside the drift of the young artist, Roderick Hudson's story in the eponymous novel by Henry James, serialized in the *Atlantic Monthly* in 1875. Bender shows the way in which James's fiction participates in the ongoing debate over human body represented in statues, and over moral and aesthetic purity. He finds the source of the nineteenth-century tourist gaze (with its taste for male beauty captured by James in the figure of Roderick) in the work of the eighteenth-century German art historian, Johann Joachim Winckelmann, who taught European and thus also indirectly American tourists the appropriate rhetoric of art appreciation and at the same time appreciation of male beauty. In his richly nuanced reading, Bender shows the stages of art and connoisseurship, of which the classical aesthetics of James's *Roderick Hudson* is a prime illustration.

The issues of tourist gaze and connoisseurship are given yet another turn in Chapter 5, in which Hitomi Nabae (Japan) traces the transformation of private collections into public museums as a cultural and social phenomenon. She explores the intricacies of human desire to possess in and around James's fiction. On one hand, Nabae highlights several case studies of travelling admirers and collectors of art in *Roderick Hudson* (1876), *The Portrait of a Lady* (1881), *The Spoils of Poynton* (1896), *The Golden Bowl* (1904), *The Outcry* (1911), and *The American Scene* (1907), while on the other she draws a large panorama of James's world, including such contemporaries as Isabella Stewart Gardner, whose dedication to acquiring art souvenirs was fed by a whole network of art guides and dealers, most notably Bernard Berenson or Otto Gunterkunst. In her acute perception of the scene of art market, Nabae exposes the tendency of wealthy art collectors to treat not only objects but also other people as collectibles. Their replacements and reshufflings of acquired objects, their sending of art objects and human captives on long voyages, also entail redefinitions of culture and identity.

In Chapter 6, Urszula Gołębiowska (Poland) looks at James's reengagements with the United States in *The American Scene*, "The Jolly Corner" (1908), and "A Round of Visits" (1910), following his visit to the United States in 1904 and 1905. In his fiction and non-fiction of the attempted return, space and time, home and the past, become one – an amalgam of irretrievable experiences, sights, and sounds. The narrator of *The American Scene* bewails the fact that there is no room left for non-collectible objects of the past in the industrialized urban space of building boom and mass immigration. James's birthplace in New York is gone and with it also, as he ruefully remarks, half of his history. Henry James, who had read French history from (remnants of) its architecture in *A Little Tour in France*, is twenty years later lamenting in *The American Scene* the absence of architectural landmarks of his personal history. Gołębiowska shows that conscious critical reflection has to give way to ghostly returns of the past enacted in James's late tale.

Notes

1 This project benefitted greatly from a fellowship of the Bogliasco Foundation. I am also very grateful to Professor Massimo Bacigalupo for inspiring conversations and for introducing me to Angloliguria.
2 This intriguing part of the novelist's legacy was addressed on 25 May 2018 during the session "Henry James Out West" organized by the Henry James Society at the 29th Annual Conference the American Literature Association in San Francisco. Philip Horne contributed a paper on "Henry James's Sense of the West" and Beverly Haviland discussed "A Sense of the Past that is not my own: Henry James, the American West, and Public Memory."
3 Henry James first took Lamb House on a twenty-one year lease, beginning in September 1897, but when his landlord died, he was offered "the freehold at the modest figure of £2,000" (Hyde 1966: 50). His intention was to spend in Rye especially the summer months (from May to October), but the autumns proved to be so mild in Rye that he could stay on until after Christmas or even longer. It was only in the last years of his life that "ill-health forced him . . . to spend more and more time in London" (Hyde 1966: 50).
4 *A Little Tour in France* came out in 1884, the title page was dated 1885.
5 Shawna Ross is working on the book project *Leisured Fictions: Hotels, Ocean Liners, and the Scene of Transatlantic Modernism*, which includes the work of Henry James.

Bibliography

Anderson, Quentin (1957) *The American Henry James*, New Brunswick, NJ: Rutgers University Press.

Anesko, Michael (2016) "Introduction: A Little Tour with Henry James," *Travels with Henry James*, New York: Nation Books: xv–xxiii.

Brooks, Peter (2007) *Henry James Goes to Paris*, Princeton, NJ: Princeton University Press.

Gunter, Susan E. (2009) *Alice in Jamesland: The Story of Alice Howe Gibbens James*, Lincoln and London: University of Nebraska Press.

Hertzberg, Hendrik (2016) "Foreword," *Travels with Henry James*, New York: Nation Books: v–xiii.

Hovanec, Evelyn A. (1979) *Henry James and Germany*, Amsterdam: Rodopi.

Hyde, H. Montgomery (1966) *The Story of Lamb House: The Home of Henry James*, Rye: Adams of Rye Limited.

James, Henry (1993a) *Collected Travel Writings: The Continent*, edited by Richard Howard, New York: Library of America.

——— (1993b) *Collected Travel Writings: Great Britain and America*, edited by Richard Howard, New York: Library of America.

——— (2006) *The Complete Letters of Henry James 1855–1872*, vols. 1–2, edited by Pierre A. Walker and Greg W. Zacharias, Lincoln and London: University of Nebraska Press.

——— (2014) *The Complete Letters of Henry James 1878–1880*, vol. 1, edited by Pierre A. Walker and Greg W. Zacharias, Lincoln and London: University of Nebraska Press.

Jolly, Roslyn (2010) "Travel and Tourism," *Henry James in Context*, edited by David McWhirter, Cambridge: Cambridge University Press: 343–53.

Kaplan, Fred (1992) *Henry James: The Imagination of Genius, a Biography*, New York: Morrow.

Moore, Harry T. (1974) *Henry James*, London: Thames and Hudson.

Tintner, Adeline R. (1993) *The Cosmopolitan World of Henry James: An Intertextual Study*, Baton Rouge and London: Louisiana State University Press.

Walker, Pierre A. (1995) *Reading Henry James in French Cultural Contexts*, DeKalb: Northern Illinois University Press.

Wrenn, Angus (2009) *Henry James and the Second Empire*, London: Legenda.

1 *The Ambassadors, The American Scene,* and the Transnational Turn in American Studies

Allen Hibbard

"The 'Transnational Turn,'" Donald E. Pease boldly asserts in his introduction to *Re-Framing the Transnational Turn in American Studies*, "has effected the most significant reimagining of the field of American studies since its inception" (2011: 10). Indeed, we have recently seen a wave of scholarly writing devoted to US interactions with the world, including (but certainly not limited to) work by Wai Chi Dimock, Paul Giles, Brian Edwards, Inderpal Grewal, Ramon Saldívar, Shirley Geok-lin Lim, and Walter Mignolo. The transnational, Pease writes, is "a volatile transfer point." The term denotes "a behavioral category that imputes the traits of flexibility, non-identification, hybridity and mobility to agents" (2011: 13). As such, transnational movement thus challenges and transcends strict national loyalties and affiliations. Travel, migration, and border crossings are accompanied by transformations of those migrating or travelling subjects. And with such movement, the very forms of representation (for example, novel, travelogue, autobiography, cultural critique) undergo transformation. Transnational narratives, as well as critical work on the transnational, prompt us to become more aware of cultural differences and our own relations to others beyond national borders.

The Transnational Turn in American Studies is grounded in a critique of the US position in the world, notably a critique of exceptionalist assumptions and ideologies that have often informed and shaped US international policies and attitudes. Transnational considerations place strong nativist propensities alongside more cosmopolitan views from the outside. The surge of scholarly interest and activity that has reoriented the field of American Studies is lodged within and no doubt precipitated or at least conditioned by contemporary historical circumstances – the complex and often vexed relationship between the United States and the world during this period of late empire. It must be seen, too, as at once embedding, reflecting and critiquing long-standing tensions in US politics between engagement and isolation or non-involvement, dating from as early as George Washington's Farewell

Address cautioning against permanent alliances and Thomas Jefferson's Inaugural Address laying out a policy of "no entangling alliances," stretching up to current debates over international trade policies and military intervention abroad. In literature as well as politics, nativist impulses have contended with cosmopolitan perspectives. Pease traces the development of the term "transnational" temporally from the 1960s and 1970s, at the time of the civil rights and women's movements, and resistance to the Vietnam War, becoming fully manifest in the post-Soviet period. Up through the present, the transnational dynamic has continued to evolve alongside globalization, anxieties about the position of the United States in the world, economically and militarily, the decline of the middle class, fears of immigrants and foreigners, a rise of protectionist sentiments, climate change, etc. Not surprisingly, these thematic concerns have been registered by a number of contemporary American writers who have inscribed journeys of Americans beyond national borders.

In the course of his life and work Henry James established himself as *the* cosmopolitan writer par excellence. No other major American writer (other than perhaps Paul Bowles) so thoroughly committed himself to a life abroad, making travel and expatriation central themes of his work. My purpose in this chapter is to examine James's novel *The Ambassadors*, published in 1903, and his cultural critique cum travelogue, *The American Scene*, published in 1907, through the lens of or in light of the Transnational Turn. How does a consideration of the Transnational Turn advance, deepen, or widen our understandings of these works? And, how do readings of *The Ambassadors* and *The American Scene* advance, deepen, or widen our understanding of transnational issues? *The Ambassadors* sets out a narrative and offers terms perfectly suited for an examination of the American expatriate experience, particularly an assessment of the effects and value of spending time abroad. *The American Scene*, in almost an inverse fashion, providing us, if you will, a supplement or the flip side of the coin, literally figures the return, displaying heightened critical capacities of the returning expatriate. I wish here to pursue an examination of how these issues play out in these two works – how gains and losses can be calculated, how the return figures in, and how these questions might apply to subsequent expatriate literature, within the context of changing relations between the United States and the world central to considerations associated with the Transnational Turn in American Studies.

The international theme in Henry James's work has long been recognized and discussed by critics, and recent work (for instance, John Carlos Rowe's piece on "Henry James and Globalization") has sought to place James within contemporary conversations on transnationalism and globalization. The kind of approaches associated with the Transnational Turn widens the scope of analysis to consider ways in which literary works are situated within US interactions with the world. The Transnational Turn in American Studies, along with theories of mobility and travel, makes us more attentive to the set of factors surrounding each individual experience of travel and movement, including specific political, economic, and cultural power dynamics at play. The dramatic actions in *The Ambassadors* and *The American Scene* unfold against the backdrop of US interactions with the world at the dawn of the twentieth century, just as earlier articulations of travel and life abroad – in works by James Fenimore Cooper (*The Bravo*, 1831; *The Heidenmauer*, 1832; *The Headsman*, 1833), Washington Irving (*Tales of the Alhambra*, 1832), and Nathaniel Hawthorne (*The Marble Faun*, 1860) – register and respond to particular concerns and transnational dynamics of their times. The protagonist of James's novel, Lambert Strether, journeys at a time when the United States was a vibrant, rising young nation, experiencing population growth, industrialization, an influx of immigrants, and urbanization. We must take note at the outset that James himself, like his protagonist Strether, was a beneficiary of the rise of American strength and power even while he chose to live at a distance from his homeland. And in *The American Scene* our "restored absentee" encounters a modern landscape marked by skyscrapers, immigration, and increased pace and movement.

We should note as well that the travels of James and his characters were limited to the comfortable sphere of familiar western values and civilization – not unlike the way the great medieval Arab traveller Ibn Battuta, even as he travelled broadly and extensively, remained within Dar al-Islam, a realm in which familiar beliefs and ideologies prevailed. For views from "outside" the hegemon, we must go elsewhere. Indeed, a critical appraisal of James, travel, empire, and the transnational takes note of the particular well-travelled routes he and his characters take and their relatively privileged positions, as well as regions that lie outside the scope of their journeys, along lines James Clifford attends to in his now classic study *Routes*.

In their introduction to *Globalizing American Studies*, Brian T. Edwards and Dilip Parmeshwar Gaonkar touch on the experiences of Americans abroad and suggest that examinations of the American expatriate novel can productively complicate our understanding of both the United States and the world. "What we call the *cosmopolitan strand* of American studies . . . rejects the metaphoric unity of American experience, and in its place metonymically focuses on the differential placement of America abroad," they write. "There is a fragmentedness in the figure of the American abroad that carries over to the figure of America or American forms abroad. . . . The American abroad experiences a multilateralism, so his or her report back home cannot have a unity in the way that vernacular reports, even in their diversity and multiplicity, seem to" (Edwards and Gaonkar 2010: 14–15). These observations are especially salient to James's fiction, as well as – more broadly – to American expatriate literature, as Edwards and Gaonkar suggest. Strether's experiences abroad disrupt his notions of home. Similarly, James's experiences abroad inform and disrupt his views of home when he returns to his homeland in 1904, after a couple of decades away, recorded in *The American Scene*.

One way to pursue the operation of the transnational in these two works is to revisit and assess the narratives themselves, narratives that highlight the effects of travel abroad, in ways which are at once specific yet seem to apply more broadly to the kinds of experiences we see in other American expatriate works. In *The Ambassadors* James richly explores the nature of the journey abroad and its effects on human beings, notably with respect to his American protagonist Strether. Why does he go, what happens to him, and what might his narrative symbolically say about the United States and the world? From the opening scenes of the novel (in Chester, England) to the end (in Paris), Strether experiences an exhilarating and sometimes dizzying expansion of being and consciousness, prompted by his exposure to new scenes, cultures, and manners. The narrative structure thus follows the pattern of a travelogue. In this process we witness an erosion of his commitment to the mission he was sent on (to bring home Chad Newsome so he can take advantage of business opportunities) as he succumbs to the pleasures and temptations of life abroad, particularly in Paris. Strether's loyalties shift, departing from and transcending the interests of the party who sent him on his mission, Mrs. Newsome, as he takes things in and sees another (transnational) perspective, adjusting his own moral compass and views in response to his apprehension of fresh and changing circumstances. He thus renounces the original task that had been entrusted to him, becoming – perhaps – a less than effective ambassador. Then, in the end, we seem to have – possibly – another renunciation, a reversal of his first renunciation. "Then there we are!" Strether famously exclaims in the last line of the novel. Yet, as is so typical in James, it is not entirely clear just where we are.

The reader, the critic, is left to assess what Strether has gained and lost through his venture, to reflect on the value of his transnational experience. Throughout the novel, as we travel looking over Strether's shoulder, we witness a quickening of our protagonist's sensibilities as he encounters new geographies, manners, and customs. The famous description of Strether's experience in Gloriani's garden, in Book V, is exemplary: "Strether, in contact with that element as he had never yet so intimately been, had the consciousness of opening to it, for the happy instant, all the windows of his mind, of letting this rather grey interior drink in for once the sun of a clime not marked by his old geography" (James *A* 1964: 120). Above all, it is the apprehension of difference, particularly between Woollett, Massachusetts, his place of residence in the United States, and Paris, that prompts a widening of his views, from the difference between the yellow covers of books in Paris and the green covers of the Woollett journal Strether had edited, to the difference in the values ascribed to relationships, be they "virtuous" or otherwise. All of this Strether takes in. Upon meeting Little Bilham and Miss Barrace for breakfast soon after he arrives in Paris, we are told: "It was interesting to him to feel that he was in the presence of new measures, other standards, a different scale of relations, and that evidently here were a happy pair who didn't think of things at all as he and Waymarsh thought" (James *A*: 77). In Paris, we are told at another point, he is exposed to a range of points of view while in Woollett, there were just three or four (James *A*: 109).

Thus develops Strether's sense of a "double consciousness," a condition of being here and there at once, comparing values of one place to those of another, resulting in an expansion of self, a move toward a more cosmopolitan perspective, one that admits that in other places people do things differently and believe different things. Travel is the vehicle by which these new perspectives are achieved. Key here, for Strether, are questions of knowledge. In Woollett he knew the codes and had a comfortable understanding of things around him; here in this new place he finds himself surrounded by new facts and relations he must strive to understand. "He was moving verily in a strange air and on ground not of the firmest," we are told in one place (James *A*: 158); in another that he was "moving in a maze of mystic closed allusions" (James *A*: 165). These sometimes fumbling attempts to figure out what is going on around him are especially apparent as Strether tries to discern Madame de Vionnet's motives with Chad. He finds the woman so intriguing precisely because she is an enigma, because he cannot read her well. In the famous scenes in the French countryside, late in the novel, his preconceived ideas collide with another kind of truth, right before his eyes: the image of Chad and Madame de Vionnet together in the boat, suggesting a kind of intimacy he had not, until then, apprehended so palpably and directly. He then, after taking in these new meanings, must adjust his views – the age-old move from innocence or naïveté to experience, a quality that, like his brother William – following Emerson – James placed great stock in. This radical reorientation of perspective in the face of freshly perceived realities often accompanies the transnational experience.

If Strether's gains include a wider moral vision, a greater range of freedom, and a quickening of the imagination, on the other side of the balance sheet he loses a sense of financial security and stability. It is the familiar trade-off between time and money, obligation and freedom. Strether, in the end, insists that he get nothing out of his venture, that he not profit financially, or be beholden to others' interests. "Poor Strether" becomes not only someone who might deserve our pity, our sympathy; he also becomes a man with uncertain financial prospects. To do Mrs. Newsome's bidding, and be an effective emissary – to bring Chad home – certainly would have resulted in a gain for him (perhaps even, it is implied, marriage to Mrs. Newsome). "Are you, my dear man, *dished*?" Chad exclaims to Strether in Book XI. Indeed he likely is. He has renounced not only possibilities back home, with Mrs. Newsome, but also with Maria Gostrey, as well.

I pick up here on the thinking of Ross Posnock in his recent book *Renunciation*. Both Strether and Chad (as well as their creator) are renunciators *par excellence*, giving up homeland, putting their means of support at risk. Theirs is the kind of "generative" renunciation Posnock describes and finds so fascinating. There is less at stake for Chad Newsome than for Strether, however, as he prolongs his stay in Paris. As a member of the Newsome family Chad enjoys a secure financial position, though apparently there are prospects of greater gain if he were to come home and take advantage of opportunities. The grandness of one's renunciation, it seems, is determined by the degree of risk one takes, the extent of what one gives up. While Strether does not have a lot to give up (in comparison, say, to Chad), other than prospects, he gives up a great deal of the little he has.

Renunciation, here, for Strether, involves cutting or at least loosening ties to country, acquaintances, and previous loyalties, reassessments and renunciations engendered by the transnational experience. Strether's position conforms to Pease's articulation: "The transnational is an inherently split subject position embroiled in the transnational/diaspora complex" (2016: 57). This splitting brings the subject in contact with the diasporic figure, insofar as the transnational subject (in this case Strether) experiences a rupture from nation/state (in this case Mrs. Newsome), left adrift, in a condition similar to (but by no means identical to) diasporic subjects. Strether's realignment of loyalties, as he frees himself from obligations to Mrs. Newsome and to home, symbolically displays that element key to transnational movement, a transcendence of purely national concerns and interests, an awareness that there are other valid subject positions. The novel also reveals the kinds of mechanisms used by those in power (for example, Mrs. Newsome) to gain and maintain loyalty: money (financial aid!), threats, coercion, and granting or withholding opportunities. Her tactics are not so unlike those used by powerful states to get less-powerful states to do their bidding, or side with them.

This whole experience of travel or expatriation thus can have a profound effect, at once disorienting and mind-expanding. My contention is that Strether does not end up where he began; he comes out somewhere else, as difficult as it may be to say for sure just where that is. (It might be that in the end he is in some kind of floating world, akin perhaps to a condition of Kantian disinterestedness.) What he has gained is experience, aesthetic experience, precipitated by travel and exposure to other cultures. An ultimate tallying of the balance sheet is necessarily inconclusive. Indeed, it necessarily challenges notions of certainty. A forsaking or renunciation of monetary gain is compensated by the acquisition of aesthetic experience, with a value that exceeds the bounds of any strictly economical calculation. That opening into the aesthetic realm is most vividly seen in the famous country scene (Book XI, sc. iii) when Strether recalls the Lambinet painting he could not buy earlier in his life. Travelling by train through the French countryside he is reminded of a painting he "*would* have bought," had the price not been out of his reach (James *A*: 301). The scene brings into play so many key aspects of the novel: experience, a sense of belatedness, freedom from responsibility, financial means, the making and framing of art. What value can be placed on the sublime experience, the beautiful work of art?

Ultimately the question is "What is the *return*"—invoking both the notion of the return on one's investment as well as a return home? That question we might link to an appraisal of travel in general as well as to Strether's particular experience, recounted in James's novel, or James's own prolonged stay abroad. It is nearly always assumed, in discussions of the transnational, that there is some benefit attached to that move beyond one's national borders. Yet, what is it? How do we determine it? In years following the publication of *The Ambassadors*, James extends and deepens his treatment of these questions, in response to his return to the United States, after an uninterrupted period of more than two decades abroad, a return that resulted in his remarkable book *The American Scene* and his story "The Jolly Corner." The return – James's own return – was accompanied by sharp observations of differences between the country he had known in his youth and a country in the throes of tremendous growth, development, and change. Indeed, there *was* a tangible return on his experiences abroad, in the form of a broadened vision as well as in literary production.

As in *The Ambassadors*, it is travel that precipitates, propels, and shapes the structure of *The American Scene*. Indeed, *The American Scene* stands as a unique instance of the travel book. Considering the work alongside the novel enriches our understanding of the integral place of travel for James (as topic, motivating force, and organizing principle), and more broadly the connections between travel writing and fiction. James brings to his treatment of the United States the same kind of open consciousness and readiness of apprehension that his protagonist Strether brings to his encounters with England and France. The difference – and it is an important one at that – is that he now turns a critical eye on his homeland, after a long period of absence, analogous to the experience of Rip Van Winkle who wakes up after a decades long sleep to find the familiar landscape around him radically transformed by intervening events, most notably a revolutionary overthrow of English rule in favor of a new democratic form of government. As such, thus, *The American Scene*, while dependent on travel, falls as much or more within the category of cultural critique, blurring generic categories. James, the returning, loving critic, brings to his assessment of the United States a different measure, beyond that of a strictly nativist perspective. As Leon Edel puts it in his introduction to the work: "His eye had become almost as fresh as that of inquiring strangers." Yet, as Edel goes on to note, "he had the advantage of not being a stranger" (Edel 1968: vii).

Edel reminds us that James had already shown himself to be an inveterate traveller and perceptive travel writer, as seen in *English Hours*, *Italian Hours*, and *A Little Tour in France*. In those travel writings, as will be seen in other essays in this volume, James, propelled by a sense of romance, was drawn to the picturesque, to landscapes imbued with a rich sense of the past. Europe was new, fresh, and different. Now, upon the author's return, entering the seventh decade of his life, America was surrounded with an uncanny air of romance. It was a place he had known, but time had in places transformed the landscape. This sense of romance especially blossoms during his travels through the South. In his chapter on Richmond, he writes:

> The European complexity, working clearer to one's vision, had grown usual and calculable – presenting itself, to the discouragement of wasteful emotion and of "intensity" in general, as the very stuff, the common texture, of the real world. Romance and mystery – in other words the *amusement* of interest – would have therefore at last to provide for themselves elsewhere; and what curiously befell, in time, was that the native, the forsaken scene, now passing, as continual rumour had it, through a thousand stages and changes, and offering a perfect iridescence of fresh aspects, seemed more and more to appeal to the faculty of wonder. . . . Nothing could be of a simpler and straighter logic: Europe had been romantic years before, because she was different from America; wherefore American would now be romantic because she was different from Europe.
>
> (James *AS* 1968: 366)

The trajectory of *The American Scene* follows the path of a journey, moving from New York, New Jersey, New England, Boston, New England, Newport, Philadelphia, Baltimore, Concord, DC, Charleston, and – finally – Florida. The itinerary of James's actual tour is slightly reconfigured in the narrative, to iron out overlaps, and create a more harmonious structure. The object of our returning expatriate is to see as clearly as possible realities lying before him in the United States and find a language (often highly figural) to represent what he takes in. He serves as a kind of Emersonian "transparent eyeball," if you will. Like Strether, the restless analyst becomes an interpreter of signs. What do things represent? For instance, upon observing the "cult of candy" prevalent in the country, he takes the next step, asking "What does it mean?" This epistemological process involves, at times, the operation of memory, as well as keenly seeing and "listening" to what things are "saying" – in ways resembling Heideggerian hermeneutics. What do things give back? How much of what one apprehends resides in the thing itself, and how much is constructed subjectively by the observer? Ceaselessly, our restless analyst looks for interest, and ways of sustaining interest. And here one cannot help thinking of the rich financial connotations associated with "interest" and "return." Interest adds value to one's investment. Without interest there would be no increase of value. Matters of money thus figure prominently in *The American Scene*, just as they do in *The Ambassadors*.

And, just as Strether measures his experiences in Europe against what he has known in the United States, our astute travelling critic measures his experiences comparatively – this time comparing the United States to Europe. Once again, transnational perspectives come into play. Values are seen and assessed in *relation* (such a key term for James). We see this comparativist mode of perception, for instance, in his reading of the Boston Public Library, "the Florentine palace by Copley Square": "Our impression here, once more, that every one is 'in' everything, whereas in Europe so comparatively few persons are in anything (even as yet in 'society,' more and more the common refuge or retreat of the masses)" (James *AS* 1968: 249). It is, he determines, "an institution without 'penetralia,' doors open with broad access, producing a hustle and bustle – like a railway station! Our returning critic is shocked to find art – Sargent and others – hung in this vulgar setting (James *AS* 1968: 251)! Similarly, in his examination of Washington, DC, he compares the Capitol dome to St. Peter's in Rome, admiring the monument erected to house and commemorate essential principles of government. Not unlike St. Peter's in Rome, sitting beside the "yellow Potomac" just as St. Peter's lies beside "the like-coloured Tiber," our critic finds the Capitol capable "of admirable, of sublime, effects" (James *AS* 1968: 360).

While our restless analyst realizes and embraces positive and promising aspects of the American scene, as he weighs and measures, putting United States beside Europe, the United States often comes up short. Here in America he sees a "thinness" compared to a "thickness" in Europe. Here he finds a plasticity, there – rigidity. Here, flux; there, order. To a great extent the deficiencies of his native land lie in its lack of a rich and storied past, as well as little indication of or planning for a future. Even much earlier, we may recall, in his biography of Hawthorne, James had famously offered a critique of America – its slim literary tradition a reduced capacity to cultivate great works of art – that formed a compelling rationale for his move abroad. The primary cultural value, associated with modernity, seemed to be movement itself. Places that hold most interest for the returning pilgrim are those imbued with memories, places where things had happened in the past and had been recorded. Concord is enriched by memories of Emerson and Thoreau. Mount Vernon is infused with the presence of George Washington.

A sense of poverty and deficiency is also felt on aesthetic grounds as our expatriate writer returns from Europe and encounters his homeland afresh. So often absent from the picture is a sense that care has been taken to please the eye. One of the few moments our critic feels the kind of thrill Strether experiences when he takes in the French countryside scene and thinks of the Lambinet painting is on his visit to Sunnyside, Washington Irving's sleepy old domicile, so harmoniously nestled within the natural landscape. So much of what he sees is marred by vulgar effects of modernity: railroads cutting through a landscape, skyscrapers jaggedly scratching the skyline, roaring motor cars and masses of foreign faces crowding the streets. His is certainly a sensibility that privileges "things sifted and selected," the very principle of art itself (James *AS* 1968: 252).

Questions of aesthetic value raised in *The Ambassadors*, thus, are further pursued and probed in *The American Scene*, where our returning absentee is assaulted by the preponderant force of *money*, the dominant and propelling cultural force apparent in the United States, registered frequently in his critical study, particularly, it seems, during his visits to and meditations on New York, a city where money seems to rule, above all else. There is much to admire in the display of zeal, energy, ambition, all with a seemingly boundless sense of space, moving upward and sprawling outward. And certainly, he notes, there are striking examples (the Gardner Museum in Boston, the Metropolitan Museum in New York) of money being used philanthropically for the public good, acquiring works of cultural value to be shared more widely. But the relentless engine behind all of this, the primacy of commerce, trade, and accumulation as key motives for doing things, informing the arrangement of things, remained a vexing matter.

A key question for James in *The American Scene* is: Why has not the drive to acquire money not been accompanied by a cultivation of aesthetic appreciation, particularly with all the essential raw materials on hand? Characteristic are his gaping responses to the incredible wealth displayed in New York and the uses to which it is put:

> The effect of certain of the manifestations of wealth in New York is, so far as I know, unique; nowhere else does pecuniary power so beat its

wings in the void, and so look round it for the charity of some hint as
to the possible awkwardness or possible grace of its motion, some sign
of whether it be flying, for good taste, too high or too low. . . . I found
myself recognizing in the New York predicament a particular character
and a particular pathos. The whole costly up-town demonstration was
a record, in the last analysis, of individual loneliness; whence came,
precisely, its insistent testimony to waste – waste of the still wider sort
than the mere game of rebuilding.

(James *AS* 1968: 159)

Given all the advantages with which his homeland was blessed, the presence of all the elements that should or could go into the making of aesthetic
value, it had not *yet* happened. What would it take? "If with so many of the
conditions they [these blessings] yet hang back, on what particular occult
furtherance must they not incorruptibly depend?" our restless analyst asks.
"Entrancing speculation!" (James *AS* 1968: 447). It might ultimately come
down to a matter of care, he speculates, a speculation, like any financial
speculation, that may or may not lead to a profitable outcome, a return on
his interest. "Would there be enough here?" Our travelling critic wonders as
his journey stretches out in time and space, answering tentatively with an
uneasy blend of hope and skepticism.

The attention to and concern for aesthetic values must certainly, at some
point, be linked to an attention to and concern for social and political structures. What kinds of societies produce substantial, vibrant, lasting art? His
return to the United States brings him up squarely against notions of democracy, which he is now able to see *in relation* to his experience abroad, as a
result of his transnational moves. One effect of a democratic social order is
a levelling, producing a reduced range of types. Another effect, it seems,
is an inherent difficulty, with competing factions, to agree upon fixed purposes, particularly when every citizen considers it his or her right to pursue life, liberty and happiness (read: making money) as he or she pleases.
An ultimate tallying of the success or failure of democracy as a social and
political form is, for James, still an open question. He registers his thoughts
in remarks on the nation's capital.

It comes back to what we constantly feel, throughout the country, to
what the American scene everywhere depends on for half of its appeal
or its effect; to the fact that the social conditions, the material, pressing
and pervasive, make the particular experiment or demonstration, whatever it may pretend to, practically a new and incalculable thing. . . .
The thing is happening, or will have to happen, in the American

way – that American way which is more different from all other native ways, taking country with country, than any of these latter are different from each other; and the question is of how, each time, the American way will see it through.

(James AS 1968: 357)

Here James certainly recognizes a peculiar American character and philosophy, distinct from other countries. Yet, he defers conclusions, unwilling yet to proclaim the United States an unqualified success. He sees the American social, political project as an experiment, still unfolding. He displays, as Ross Posnock emphasizes in his fine essay on *The American Scene*, a "preference for open questions" (Posnock 1998: 225). As the writer takes in and reflects on our nation's capital, he wonders: "What therefore will the multitudinous and elaborate forms of the Washington to come have to 'say,' and what, above all, besides gold and silver, and marble and trees and flowers, will they be able to say it *with*? That is one of the questions in the mere phrasing of which the restless analyst finds a thrill" (James *AS* 1968: 358). He sounds this note again, as he visits Richmond, the capital of the old, now defunct Confederacy, saying that it would be "premature" to measure and judge once and for all the results of the US experiment. Rather, in ways reminiscent of Thoreau (in "Resistance to Civil Government") and more recently Derrida, James leaves open the prospects of a "democracy to come":

Of all the solemn conclusions one feels as "barred," the list is quite headed, in the States, I think, by this particular abeyance of judgment. When an ancient treasure of precious vessels, overscored with glowing gems and wrought artistically, into wondrous shapes, has, by a prodigious process, been converted, through a vast community, into the small change, the simple circulating medium of dollars and "nickels," we can only say that the consequent permeation will be of values of a new order. Of *what* order we must wait to see.

(James AS 1968: 382)

The point to be underscored here, as we view these works through the lens of recent work in transnational studies, is that the view from the outside almost necessarily is accompanied by a questioning of US exceptionalism. The American experiment, novel and intriguing as it is, is subject to skeptical appraisal, criticisms that expose contradictions between ideals and realities. There are other ways of human organization, other means in which things can be arranged.

Coming toward the end of his tour, or at least the book containing his attempts to come once again to "know" and account for his homeland, our restless analysis finds himself in a place not unlike Strether at the end of *The Ambassadors* – adrift.

> One had already, in moving about, winced often enough at sight of where one was, intellectually, to "land," under these last consistencies of observation and reflection; so I may put it that I *didn't*, after all, land, but recoiled rather and forbore, making my skiff fast to no conclusion whatever, only pushing out again and letting it, for a supreme impression and to prepare in the aftertime the best remembrance, drift where it would.
>
> (James *AS* 1968: 420–1)

James's story "The Jolly Corner" first published in 1908, unimaginable without his return to the United States, allows us to apply one more turn of the screw on themes we have been discussing here: the operation of the transnational, connections between fiction and non-fiction, and the effects and value of experience abroad. The central character in the story, Spencer Brydon, must come to a reckoning of what he is after a life abroad versus what he might have been had he stayed home. As Spencer Brydon returns to New York City after an extended sojourn abroad – to tend to business concerns, he contemplates – against the foil of a haunting double – the nature of his sacrifice and what kind of (financial) success he might have enjoyed had he stayed home and pursued a business career. "I might have put in here all these years. Then everything would have been different enough – and, I dare say, 'funny,'" he tells his interlocutor and companion, Miss Staverton (James JC 1969: 322). He goes on to say: "There are no reasons here *but* of dollars." He obsessively thinks of "how he might have led his life and 'turned out'" had he stayed at home (James JC 1969: 323). "I should have stuck here. . . . I might have been, by staying here, something nearer to one of these types who have been hammered so hard and made so keen by their conditions" (James JC 1969: 324). He might even have had a hand in the creation of skyscrapers, it is suggested. He confesses he had been living a "selfish frivolous scandalous life" the past thirty years away from home. Yet, at the same time he imagines that his alter ego, the one who stayed home, could have become "hideous and offensive" (James JC 1969: 325). Miss Staverton, his confidant in the story (his Maria Gostrey, if you will), has imagined that other self twice in a dream, and suggests that he would have "had power" – perhaps a nod to the increased power of the United States during the time of Brydon's absence. He would have been shaped by the same cultural forces that so fascinated and frequently horrified our "restless analyst" in *The American Scene*. Indeed, actual visits to places he had lived in his youth, both in New York and Boston, seem to lie behind the story, indicating again a strong connection between travel and fictional representation in James.

When, finally, after a long period of nocturnal vigils in his old family home on the jolly corner, Brydon finally conjures up and "meets" his alter ego, he finds that other possible version of himself – the one who had stayed home – monstrous, and recoils, collapsing, horrified upon seeing so clearly the image, struck by the immense difference between these two selves – the one who stayed versus the one who went abroad. When, after reviving from his faint, Brydon presses Miss Staverton to tell him which version of him she would have preferred, she seems to imply that she might have loved either one, but she embraces the one before her in the end. This alter ego, as Miss Staverton notes, though he may have "a million a year," "has been unhappy; he has been ravaged" (James JC 1969: 349). As much or more than *The Ambassadors*, this late story deals squarely with a reckoning, a weighing and measuring of the value of the expatriate experience, a dramatic presentation of the difference between a life spent abroad and a life spent at home. Here, it seems, James comes to terms with whatever loss one might suffer and celebrates, in a kind of Nietzschean fashion (*amor fati*), the self his protagonist has become and now is, without resentment or regret.

As in *The Ambassadors*, the reckoning or assessment presented in "The Jolly Corner" focuses on actual, monetary loss and gain. James himself, as we know (from reading biographically based work such as that by Leon Edel and Colm Tóibín or critical studies such as Michal Anesko's *Friction with the Market*) was keenly interested in getting a return on his work, on his writing, transforming experience into a marketable product. For James, the writer, experience was not enough; it must be given form. This was James's passion, his motive for making fiction (as well as providing a means of support). For Strether, significantly, as we have seen, by contrast, there is no tangible *return* – of either sort – at least not within the pages of the novel. In the end, he is left with no particular plans, in Europe, insisting that he not profit from his experience. Indeed, there seems to be something in the very nature of profit that sullies the purity of experience. Strether doesn't even get a novel out of it – or (in a sense) perhaps he does!

Insofar as Strether comes to see and appreciate values of another culture, to apprehend difference not wholly in terms of the unrivaled supremacy of one's one culture, his journey exemplifies a key element underlying the transnational turn – that is, a challenge or critique of American exceptionalism. Yet, as suggested earlier, the circumstances of his travel as well as his identity (race, nationality, gender) to some degree constrain or determine the extent and nature of his journeying. As a white American male, subsidized by Mrs. Newsome, his travels were relatively free, comfortable, and unimpeded. Diasporic and refugee studies call our attention to the particularities of subjects who leave home, forced out by tragic circumstances, caught in camps, facing dangerous crossings, frequently lacking proper papers to cross borders and enter particular countries.[1] Despite the often sharply different circumstances surrounding various kinds of transnational movement, Donald Pease has identified a central, underlying quality associated with all such experiences: "Inherently relational, the transnational/diaspora complex involves a double move: to the inside, to core constituents of a given nation; and to an outside, where diasporic processes introduce different configurations" (Pease 2016: 43). As we have seen, this "double move" (or "double consciousness," to use James's terms) is a central feature of Strether's experience travelling abroad and sojourning in Paris, as it is for the returning expatriates in *The American Scene* and "The Jolly Corner."

Each iteration of transnational movement warrants its own critical analysis that heightens awareness of motives, means, what one leaves behind, what one hopes to gain in leaving, etc. Generations of US expatriate writers following James have faced different circumstances, be it those of the Lost Generation in the aftermath of World War I, the generation of writers (including Paul Bowles and James Baldwin) after World War II, or a current generation of writers after 9/11. In each case, there are critiques and assessments of the move abroad (continuing debates about interactions with the world, entangling alliances, etc.). Near the beginning of *The Sun Also Rises*, our narrator Jake Barnes tells Robert Cohn, when Cohn shares his wish to leave Paris and go to South America: "Listen, Robert, going to another country doesn't make any difference. I've tried all that. You can't get away from yourself by moving from one place to another. There's nothing to that" (Hemingway 1926: 19). And near the end of *Giovanni's Room*, written three decades later, our narrator David recounts remarks made by his would-be fiancée Hella who, along with his Italian lover Giovanni, has been cast aside: "Americans should never come to Europe . . . it means they never can be happy again. What's the good of an American who isn't happy?" (Baldwin 1956: 242).

These novels seem to suggest that there is something distinctly American in the choice to go abroad, that it is one permutation of that quintessential American drive to find oneself, or to start afresh, calling to mind D. H. Lawrence's characterization of the American impulse – just to get away. And they often, as just noted, offer a critique of that move and the efficacy of its underlying desires. More recent expatriate novels (I think here of Andrew Erwin's *Extraordinary Renditions*, Ben Lerner's *Leaving the Atocha Station*, and Dave Eggers' *Hologram for the King*) seem to register a changed, post 9/11 relationship between the United States and the world, in which characters by going abroad (1) are not universally welcome simply because they are American; (2) can no longer pose as innocents abroad, pressed to answer to their government's at times controversial imperialist policies (for example, the narrator in *Leaving the Atocha Station* having to answer to Bush's invasion of Iraq); and (3) are less able to escape the demands and pressures of home, and to capitalize on their experiences, no doubt to a great extent, because of a globalized, digital world and a diminishing position (morally if not militarily and economically) of the United States vis-à-vis the world.

A good example of this is the situation faced by Alan Clay in *Hologram for the King*. Clay has lost his job in a Midwest bicycle manufacturing business (Schwinn) as a result of global competition. A sense of nostalgia, even while perhaps displaced or submerged by his decision to travel abroad, to Saudi Arabia, haunts the novel. Clay – in debt and dogged by family problems – seeks a way out. Early in the novel he recounts parts of a conversation with a man on a plane who proclaims: "We've become a nation of indoor cats, he'd said. A nation of doubters, worriers, overthinkers. Thank God these weren't the kind of Americans who settled this country. They were a different breed!" (Eggers 2012: 13). The hope and expectation for gain and profit associated with his decision to go on a sales trip to Saudi Arabia are, in the end, unfulfilled. The balance sheet on his return will show a deficit. We assume that his problems will be even greater when he goes home than when he left. This kind of mood and sentiment reflects the kinds of strong and prevailing feelings that have recently been expressed so powerfully in the US political arena – a craving to regain some kind of lost stature, a sense of slipping, a desire to make America great *again* (suggesting that ground has already been lost).

A deeper exploration of the tradition of the American expatriate novel, of which James is a key figure, is just one productive line of inquiry prompted by the transnational turn. Another, which I merely suggest here and have neither the space nor the background to pursue fully, would be to consider the transnational James. Just as James's protagonists have travelled, so, too, have his texts. Indeed the range of these textual travels has been much wider than the travels of James and his characters, extending beyond Europe to Russia, Asia, Latin American, the Arab world, to all corners of the globe. Each culture, and no doubt each time period, creates its own James, translating and digesting his work within particular, established literary traditions, as pieces in the 2003 issue of *The Henry James Review* devoted to "The Global Henry James" show. There, for instance, Hitomi Nabae introduces us to the Japanese Henry James, and we learn, as well about Henry James's presence in Estonia. Some time ago one of my Ph.D. students, Karine Gavand, wrote an enlightening dissertation on the reception of Henry James in France. So, too, we might think of a Brazilian Henry James, or Indian Henry James, or Moroccan Henry James. I have in mind here Shelley Fisher Fishkin's fine essay, "Transnational Mark Twain," that sketches out a "Deep Map" of "Global Huck," as well as Wai Chi Dimock's study *Through Other Continents* that shows how works such as Thoreau's "Resistance to Civil Government" have travelled, been read, and had tremendous influence in other places and times. Such a study of James (or any other US author) would intersect with translation studies, attending to various translations of the author's work, as well as critical responses, and considerations of how the writer has (or has not) influenced literary traditions elsewhere. Becoming aware of readings from "outside," a key aspect of efforts to globalize American studies, increases our sphere of knowledge and engages us more deeply with the world, countering nativist impulses to build walls and keep things (people, ideas) within traditionally defined geographic borders of nation.

Yet another possible path of exploration, prompted by a consideration of James within a transnational context, would be to set James's literary production alongside the work of European immigrants to the United States during the same period. What connections might we make, for instance, if we read James – as Gert Buelens has done – alongside the work of Mary Antin (*The Promised Land*, 1912), or Abraham Cahan (*The Rise of David Levinsky*, 1917), Anzia Yezierska (*Bread Givers*, 1925), or even D.H. Lawrence (*St. Mawr*, 1925)? Such an exercise, involving inverse migrations or crisscrossings, would allow us to compare and contrast respective subject positions and motives for travel, as well as the kinds of work produced and contrasting visions of the United States that are revealed.

Whatever approach or approaches we might take in pursuing the transnational James, the dividends will be great as we travel with James across temporal and spatial boundaries. James travelled when, to invoke a phrase used by Evelyn Waugh, "the going was good." Travel (by ship and by horse and buggy!) may have been slow and cumbersome, yet for the American the world likely seemed open and welcoming. It did indeed seem to be an age of innocence, a kind of innocence that is hard for Americans to maintain now, no matter how hard they try. These, of course, are themes James explored more than a century ago, showing characters as they develop a growing awareness of dangers lurking "out there" (or, as is usually the case, for James, *in* there). Still, despite – or perhaps even *because* of – changed cultural dynamics and calculations associated with our own historical moment, I would propose that the value of travel and experience abroad now may be as great as ever. The potential return would be some kind of understanding of a world beyond our borders perceived increasingly as threatening and hostile. There is now, to invoke the words of Zhang Longxi, "a much greater need to open one's eyes beyond the tunnel vision of one's own group or community, and [a much greater readiness to] embrace alterity beyond one's linguistic and cultural comfort zones" (2014: 515).

Note

1 It would take a good deal of time and space to explore the vast and burgeoning fields of Diasporic and Refugee Studies. Critical studies in the area include work by Fechter and Walsh, Greenblatt, Caren Kaplan, Knott and McLoughlin, John Lie, Long and Oxfeld, Boris Nieswand, Gabriel Sheffer, Ala Sirriyeh, John Urry, Genette Verstraete, Roger Zetter, etc.

Bibliography

Anesko, Michael (1986) *Friction with the Market: Henry James and the Profession of Authorship*, Oxford: Oxford University Press.

Baldwin, James (1956) *Giovanni's Room*, New York: Dial Press.

Buelens, Gert (2005) "Absentee American and Impatient Immigrant (Re)appraising the Promised Land: Henry James and Mary Antin on the New England Scene," *American Studies in Scandinavia*, vol. 37, no. 1: 34–55.

Clifford, James (1997) *Routes: Travel and Translation in the Late Twentieth Century*, Cambridge: Harvard University Press.

Dimock, Wai Chi (2006) *Through Other Continents: American Literature Across Deep Time*, Princeton, NJ: Princeton University Press.

Edel, Leon (1968) "Introduction," *The American Scene*, edited by Henry James, Bloomington: Indiana University Press: i–xiv.

Edwards, Brian T. and Dilip Parameshwar Gaonkar, eds. (2010) *Globalizing American Studies*, Chicago: University of Chicago Press.

Eggers, Dave (2012) *A Hologram for the King*, New York: Random House.

Ervin, Andrew (2010) *Extraordinary Renditions*, Minneapolis: Coffee House.

Fishkin, Shelley Fisher (2016) "Transnational Mark Twain," *American Studies as Transnational Practice: Turning toward the Transpacific*, edited by Yuan Shu and Donald E. Pease, Hanover, NH: Dartmouth University Press: 109–38.

Gavand, Karine (2008) "The French Henry James, or Henry James Under the French Critical Gaze," Dissertation, Middle Tennessee State University.

Giles, Paul (2011) *The Global Remapping of American Literature*, Princeton, NJ: Princeton University Press.

Hemingway, Ernest (1926) *The Sun Also Rises*, New York: Charles Scribner's Sons.

James, Henry (1964) *The Ambassadors*, edited by S. P. Rosenbaum, New York: W.W. Norton.

——— (1968) *The American Scene*, introduction by Leon Edel, Bloomington: Indiana University Press.

——— (1969) "The Jolly Corner," *Eight Tales from the Major Phase*, edited by Morton Dauwen Zabel, New York: W.W. Norton. Originally published 1908.

Lawrence, D.H. (1990) *Studies in Classic American Literature*, New York: Penguin Books. Originally published 1923.

Lerner, Ben (2011) *Leaving the Atocha Station*, Minneapolis: Coffee House.

Longxi, Zhang (2014) "The Changing Concept of World Literature," *World Literature in Theory*, edited by David Damrosch, Chichester, West Sussex: Wiley Blackwell: 517–18.

Nabae, Hitomi (2003) "Translation as Criticism: A Century of James Appreciation in Japan," *Henry James Review*, vol. 24, no. 3: 250–7.

Pease, Donald E. (2016) "How Transnationalism Reconfigured American Studies," *American Studies as Transnational Practice: Turning toward the Transpacific*, edited by Yuan Shuand and Donald E. Pease, Hanover, NH: Dartmouth University Press: 39–63.

Pease, Donald E., John Carlos Rowe and Winfried Fluck, eds. (2011) *Re-Framing the Transnational Turn in American Studies*, Hanover, NH: Dartmouth University Press.

Posnock, Ross (1998) "Affirming the Alien: The Pragmatist Pluralism of *The American Scene*, *The Cambridge Companion to Henry James*, edited by Jonathan Freedman, Cambridge: Cambridge University Press.

———— (2016) *Renunciation: Acts of Abandonment by Writers, Philosophers and Artists*, Cambridge: Harvard University Press.

Rowe, John Carlos (2003) "Henry James and Globalization," *Henry James Review*, vol. 24, no. 3: 205–14.

2 The sentimental tourist in rural France

Henry James's pictures of history in *A Little Tour in France* (1884, 1900)

Ágnes Zsófia Kovács

While travelling in France, James receives a particularly vivid impression of the Roman ruins at Nîmes. The remains of the *nymphaneum*, the baths and the aqueduct, trigger his imagination and he senses "a certain contagion of antiquity in the air" (James *LT* 1993a: 198). At the end of his visit, during his stroll in a French garden, into which Roman elements have been incorporated, he falls into a kind of reverie: "it seemed to me that I touched for a moment the ancient world" (James *LT* 1993a: 200). At the same time he also creates an image of his own moment of illumination by describing himself as he looks into the eighteenth-century French fountain built on Roman foundations, making out the slabs of Roman stone at the bottom of the basin through the clean green water. He not only feels he is able to touch the ancient past but also reflects on his own ability to create a connection to the past. This image of James glimpsing traces of the past recurs throughout his travelogue and brings together a picturesque scene, imaginative reconstruction and contemplation, historical interest and illumination, architectural ruins used and shaped by posterity, and, last but not least, reference to authorship. Through the use of these elements, James's *A Little Tour in France* constitutes an attempt to create imaginative personal impressions of past moments initiated by local sights. *A Little Tour* produces a view of rural France saturated with history and serves to prove the statement that France is not Paris. James travelled for six weeks from Touraine to Provence, and the book represents his interest in French landscapes and views, Frenchness, French women, and the French past.[1]

James had first published the pieces that form *A Little Tour in France* under the title *En Provence* in the 1883 and 1884 issues of *The Atlantic Monthly*. He found a new title for the book version in his 1878 article he retitled "Rheims and Laon: A Little Tour," when he prepared it for inclusion in *Portraits and Places* in 1883. James revised the text for a new book version that came out in Boston at James R. Osgood and Company in 1884, the same year he declared travel writing was a class of composition he had left behind (Stowe 1994: 163). However, in 1900 he added a new Preface, rewrote the "Introductory," and revised wording and punctuation. This new illustrated edition came with ninety-two drawings by Joseph Pennell, and was published by Houghton in Boston for the US market and by Heinemann in London, both in 1900 (Howard 1993: 792).

The work of revision remains a key issue for Jamesians and needs to be considered in connection with the two editions of *A Little Tour* as well. Philip Horne investigated the role of Jamesian revision in *The New York Edition* and claimed that James practised revision "as a respectful continuity" (1990: 154), a kind of explication replete with dialogue rather than a work of deletion and correction. Yet, Jamesian revision is not a chance explication, as David McWhirter explained when he characterized the relation between the original and the revised in James as a basically ethical act, as if "keeping the promise of the words he gave long ago" (McWhirter 1997: 159). Oliver Herford has traced James's revisions of his essays between *Transatlantic Sketches* (1883) and *Italian Hours* (1909) with a focus on the deletions of the word "picturesque" in the later version. But, Herford writes, James "allows overtones to remain there, as though it was just as a word that 'picturesque' was objectionable, and not as a sign for a collection of cultural associations" (2016: 153). Herford goes on to assert that "the alterations of emphasis manifest strengthened loyalty to picturesque surfaces" (2016: 163) as the deletions and replacements of the word reflect on the multiple meanings "picturesque" still has for James in 1909.

The imaginative reconstruction of a place to create a visual impression of it in words is a characteristically Jamesian scenario of the imaginative act[2] that remains a concern during revision, too. The work of editing in *A Little Tour* in 1900 did not involve the deletion of "picturesque" the way it happened in the case of *Italian Hours*. Rather, revision added a special focus to the pictorial aspect. James reflects on his pictorial method explicitly in his 1900 Preface to *A Little Tour*, where he defines his writing as "governed by the pictorial spirit" (James *LT* 1993a: 3). He calls his reports a string of impressions, "sketches on 'drawing paper'" (James *LT* 1993a: 3). In the third and final paragraph of the short Preface, he voices his regret that he has not spoken more or differently about France. He assumes that it must have been the depth of involvement that prevented a clearer articulation: "There are relations that soon get beyond all merely showy appearances of value for us. Their value becomes thus private and practical, and is represented by the process – the quieter, mostly, the better – of absorption and assimilation of what the relation has done for us" (James *LT* 1993a: 4). He feels he wrote little about his relation to France compared to how much he had been shaped by it. As if illustrating Horne's idea of revision to show "continuity" and McWhirter's view of an "ethical relation," between old and new versions, in *A Little Tour* the picturesque method of writing about travel is related to Jamesian aesthetics in general: the late James seems to regret the lack of "artistic" penetration on the part of his younger self.

"Pictures" in *A Little Tour* are related to past eras and reveal a historical continuity that remains central in both editions of the text. This chapter aims at explicating a spectrum of the meaning of these "pictures." Despite James's later claim to the contrary, there is a pervading interest in historical relations behind the surface the sketches show. In particular, young James develops a preference for three specific historical eras important for the French countryside. Firstly, travelling in the French South, he is impressed by the ruins of the Gallo-Roman past. Secondly, he investigates traces of the French Middle Ages in cathedrals and castles. Thirdly, he appreciates the work of the French Renaissance: palaces, tombs, and domestic architecture. He abhors the destruction the French Revolution left behind.

The role of the past in James's non-fiction in general and in *A Little Tour* in particular has been interpreted in contrasting ways. Tony Tanner writes about a wilful lack of history in James's travel texts: "[t]here is precious little history, as conventionally understood, in James's travel writing. One will look invariably in vain for a date, a fact, increasingly even a name" (1995: 12). Tanner considers this "crucial to James's original transformation of the genre" (1995: 12) as instead of facts James is looking for pleasure in the differences (Kermode 1999: 61). Nicola Bradbury agrees with Tanner that the process of imaginative reconstruction is more important for James than historical fact in his non-fiction about France (2004:188). By contrast, Herford lists the historical as one out of many strands of meaning related to the "picturesque" (2016: 164. In a similar but more explicit gesture, Eric Haralson and Kendall Johnson end their useful summary by asserting that *A Little Tour* "is especially marked by James's continual . . . realisation of the violent history of France" (2009: 355). They pinpoint James's unfaltering interest in the Enlightenment and in the enormous cultural destruction the French Revolution caused (Haralson and Johnson 2009: 356).

This chapter looks into how historical reflection is related to picturesque presentation in the book and argues that mental images of places are always related to a sense of history in Jamesian descriptions of rural and small-town France. James often relies on architecture as the source of picturesque images in order to create a sense of the past that he verbalizes for the readers. The illuminated impressions of the past in *A Little Tour* most often arise during the contemplation of buildings. This is no coincidence in a travelogue, but there are at least two major added reasons for the systematic architectural imagery. Firstly, it manifests Ruskin's habit of precise observation (Benert 1996: 325). Secondly, for the New York elite James belonged to, "France in particular represented the standard in landscapes, public places, and domestic spaces" (Benert 1996: 324). This method has been used in interpretations of *The American Scene* and can be expanded to include *A Little Tour*. Tamara Follini argues that James "organizes his memories of the American past and his critique of the American present" around architectural sites in *The American Scene* (2014: 28). One example for this process is the way he identifies features of consumer culture with the visual ugliness of skyscrapers (Buitenhuis 1957: 320). This chapter focuses on how architecture functions as the memory of the French past for James[3] in his picturesque representations of rural France in the late nineteenth century.

Self-definitions by the sentimental tourist

A Little Tour begins with a proposition it intends to demonstrate for US tourists that Paris does not equal France. Beside Paris, central France is just as interesting, the country around Tour with the Loire valley called Touraine especially, because it offers a view of the glittering times of the Monarchy with its cultivated fields and gallery of architectural specimens (James *LT* 1993a: 20). So is Southern France, the book illustrates, asserting at the end that the "proposition has been demonstrated" (James *LT* 1993a: 273).

The narrator looks for glimpses that leave "a picture in my mind" (James *LT* 1993a: 249), and this interest is defined as the "picturesque method" (James *LT* 1993a: 183) in opposition to Stendhal's travel writing, which presents no image, no colour and hence reads like an "account by a commercial traveller" (James *LT* 1993a: 183). In contrast to Stendhal, James attempts to "render the superficial aspects of things" (James *LT* 1993a: 184). His picturesque method aims at exploring the spectacle and not at creating a classification. Similarly, he enjoys a visual surprise, "those accidents in the hope of which the traveller with a propensity for sketching (either on a little paper-bloc or on the tablets of his brain) decides to turn a corner at a venture" (James *LT* 1993a: 103).

The narrator calls himself a sentimental tourist (James *LT* 1993a: 243), as he intends to capture emotions triggered by the picturesque views he finds. The term is obviously a reference to Laurence Sterne's *A Sentimental Journey through France and Italy* (1768), an extremely popular travel account in the hundred years before James's publication. In Sterne, "sentimental" serves as the opposite of classical learning and objective point of view. It refers to the need for subjective discussions of personal taste, an interest in manners and morals rather than facts (Sterne 1774: 13–14). In this vein, in view of Carcassonne, James records a great emotion (James *LT* 1993a: 160) and calls it "the best quality that a reader may hope to extract from a narrative in which 'useful information' and technical lore . . . are completely absent" (James *LT* 1993a: 160). The sentimental tourist is the opposite of someone who is out for a general description, a coherent view (James *LT* 1993a: 228), useful information, technical lore (James *LT* 1993a: 160), or facts and figures (James *LT* 1993a: 167).

James Buzard calls James's frequent use of the word "picturesque" an addiction (1993: 196) that involves parody (1993: 225) of previous touristy accounts. Peter Rawlings points to the grotesque when he argues that James revels in pictures of "ugliness, deviation, decay, deformity, and ruin, in addition to things foreign and strange," which "are at the centre of ideas of the picturesque at the end of the eighteenth century" (2004: 176). This sense of the picturesque recalls John Ruskin's distinction between noble picturesque and surface picturesque in his essay on Turner (Rawlings 2004: 178). The grotesque signals an interest in the Ruskinian surface picturesque, which also tallies with James's critical attitude towards Ruskin, who prefers the other "noble" kind of picturesque (Rawlings 2004: 178). There is certainly a good amount of tragedy and brutality involved in the impressions James's picturesque scenes invoke, but it is also possible to account for these as part of James's interest in history.

For the sentimental tourist the picturesque scene provides the major point of interest, and he calls the visual input complete with an emotional effect, or an "impression" (James *LT* 1993a: 230, 190, and 130).[4] The sentimental tourist takes time to let his impressions of places sink in: he searches for picturesque spots, records their emotional effects, and seeks to come away with "a full impression" (James *LT* 1993a: 230). At the end of the note on Le Mans, there is an excellent example of how a happy impression of a place is created. After spending the day in town, James was sitting at a café before dinner, enjoying a typical French view, when he "felt a charm, a kind of sympathy, a sense of the completeness of French life and of the lightness and brightness of the social air, together with a desire to arrive at friendly judgments, to express a positive interest. I know not why this transcendental mood should have descended on me then and there" (James *LT* 1993a: 112).

Another kind of impression takes in not only the picturesqueness of a place, but also recreates a sense of the past connected to it. At Villeneuve, "the pictorial sweetness . . . made a particular impression on me . . . of the human composition of the Middle Ages" (James *LT* 1993a: 238–40). Chambord is also suffused with history. The ruins of the castle create an impression of desolation inflicted on the place by a series of historical incidents from Revolution through Restoration to Republic. The view of the place is coupled with the story of the unfortunate Duke of Bordeaux, later Comte de Chambord, prospective king of France as Henry V. In 1870 France lost the

Franco-Prussian War, Restoration seemed possible, and the Count of Chambord was offered the throne. He would have been accepted and ordained as king had he not written his letter demanding to use the Fleur de Lys instead of the Tricolor on July 5, 1871. He was never to be king after this, and the Third Republic was established. Instead of providing an informative punchline, James offers a personal impression and a lesson of history:

> [Chambord] spoke, with a muffled but audible voice, of the vanquished monarchy, which had been so strong, so splendid, but today had become a vision almost as fantastic as the cupolas and chimneys that rose before me. I thought, while I lingered there, of all the fine things it takes to make up such a monarchy; how one of them is the superfluity of mouldering, empty palaces. Chambord is touching – that is the best word for it; and if the hopes of another restoration are in the follies of the Republic, a little reflection on that eloquence of a ruin ought to put the Republic on its guard. A sentimental tourist may venture to remark that in the presence of all the haunted houses that appeal in this mystical manner to the retrospective imagination it cannot afford to be foolish.
>
> (James *LT* 1993a: 57)

The palace reduced to a ruin reflects changes in French history. The Revolution scattered only the furnishings, but the real damage was inflicted during the Restoration and the Third Republic. The sentimental tourist forms an impression of the past glory of the Monarchy and the series of upheavals: the Monarchy was vanquished by the Revolution, the Revolution by Napoleon, Napoleon by the Restoration, and the Restoration by the Republic. This retrospective imagination cannot be content with trying to see what the past must have been like, but also considers how the past is relevant to the present time.

The picturesque method of *A Little Tour in France*, acknowledged by James both in his text of 1884 and in the Preface of 1900, opens up questions related to representation of history. A picturesque view that is colourful and charming provokes an imaginative engagement in the spectator, a moment of reflection or illumination. The analysis of impressions has revealed that the feelings produced are always impressions of the past initiated by mental pictures of architecture and linked to the present.

Architecture as the memory of history

History usually comes alive for James in the form of architectural imagery. The examples of Nîmes and Chambord have already allowed a glimpse of this method. This section looks at the way history is represented in *A Little*

Tour in order to find out how the architectural descriptions are related to the picturesque method. The question now is no longer how the picturesque method works but, more specifically, how the representations of the past are related to architectural images in the book.

In his accounts James manifests a definite interest in events of French history, two of which he finds fundamentally important. He writes that in France one encounters two great historical facts, "one is the Revolution and other is the German invasion" (James *LT* 1993a: 22). The difference between them hinges upon the traces they have left. The destruction of the Revolution remains visible. As James travels around, he encounters its horrible work first at Tours, where the entire Church of St. Martin was demolished by it (James *LT* 1993a: 32), and then at Blois, where the statue of Louis XII had been destroyed (James *LT* 1993a: 46). By Les Baux, viewing the shell of an abbey wiped out by the Revolution, James exclaims: "wherever one goes, in France, one meets, looking backward a little, the spectre of the great Revolution; and one meets it always in the shape of the destruction of something beautiful and precious. To make us forgive it at all, how much it also must have destroyed that was more hateful than itself!" (James *LT* 1993a: 226). He not only admires the church of Brou, as Matthew Arnold did, but also wonders how it survived the Revolution (James *LT* 1993a: 261, 266). At Arles, he is surprised that the Romanesque church has an uninjured porch with an embroidery of sculpture, the "one good mark for the French Revolution" (James *LT* 1993a: 220).

Another example of his view of the Revolution is articulated at Nantes, where a row of seventeenth-century houses reminds him of the executions of several hundred men and women who were thrown into the river to die. His imagination fills the eighteenth-century streets with the figures of those tortured by the Revolution:

> The tall eighteenth-century house, full of the *air noble*, in France always reminds me of these dreadful years – of the street scenes of the Revolution. Superficially, the association is incongruous, for nothing could be more formal and decorous than the patent expression of these eligible residences. But whenever I have a vision of prisoners bound on tumblers that jolt slowly to the scaffold, of heads carried on pikes, of groups of heated *citoyennes* shaking their fists at closed coach-windows, I see in the background the well-ordered features of the architecture of the period.
>
> (James *LT* 1993a: 122)

The "noble" city house reminds James of the atrocities of the Revolution that paradoxically resulted from ideas of the Enlightenment. For him this house functions as the memento of the Revolution's brutality. In contrast to the Revolution, the marks of the second historical fact, the war in 1870, have disappeared. James admires the French nation's ability to "dress her wounds" (James *LT* 1993a: 22) and go on. So while the Revolution has left traces of cultural rupture difficult to pass or renovate, the marks of the Franco-Prussian War have been cleared from view, as the French spirit to heal and gloss over ruptures prevails.

James also shows an interest in places as settings for famous historical events and in historical characters who inhabited those places. He admires the castle of Blois for "the palace is a course of French history" (James *LT* 1993a: 47), and Chenonceaux because it is "packed with history . . . of a private and sentimental kind" (James *LT* 1993a: 70). By private and senti-mental history he means the life and loves of its famous proprietors: Francis I, Henry II, Diana of Poitiers, Catherine de' Medici (James *LT* 1993a: 71). At Poitiers, he tells stories of Jeanne Darc [sic!], Charles VII, and the Black Prince (James *LT* 1993a: 138, 140), while looking in vain for a sign of the Battle of Poitiers. At Toulouse, he retells "one of the most interesting and touching episodes of the social history of the eighteenth century" (James *LT* 1993a: 158) when a Protestant father was accused of having killed his son who had Catholicized, and was tortured and executed. Voltaire investigated the case and pursued the reversal of judgement, and the father was cleared of charges posthumously (James *LT* 1993a: 159). One of James's favourite historical characters seems to be Anne of Brittany, whose life he encounters at several towns during his travels. For the first time, she is mentioned on account of the beautiful Renaissance tomb of her children at Saint Gatien of Tours (James *LT* 1993a: 28), then also at Nantes, where she was born, at Langeais, where she married her first husband Charles VIII, at Amboise, where she lost him, and at Blois, where she married her second husband, the good Louis XII, and where she herself died (James *LT* 1993a: 123).

Beside stories of historical characters, stories of authors and fictional characters accompany the descriptions of places to enhance the private nature of French history represented in *A Little Tour in France*. At the out-set of his journey, James hunts Tours for locations connected to Balzac and to his characters from "Le Curé le Tours" (James *LT* 1993a: 25). James's dislike of the lowly house in which Balzac was born is balanced by the assertion that Balzac was "a product of a soil into which a good deal of his-tory had been trodden" (James *LT* 1993a: 22, 24), Balzac obviously being the plant growing out of this soil, bearing the fruit of books rich with his-tory. Angoulême is another attractive place to visit for the sake of Balzac's characters from *Les Illusion Perdues*, who, as James argues, "have not the vagueness of identity which is the misfortune of historical characters; they are real, supremely real, thanks to their affiliation to the great Balzac, who had invented an artificial reality which was . . . better than the real article"

(James *LT* 1993a: 141). At Tarascon, he refers to Daudet, whose comic story about Provencal character rebellious against fact (James *LT* 1993a: 204) is set there. James reports the natives' displeasure at Daudet's representation of them, but he contends that Tarasconians were bright, easy, and amiably indifferent when he visited. For James, fictional figures add interest to buildings the same way as historical characters do.

In James's discussions of past events and characters, architecture is introduced as the memory of the past. At Nîmes, James senses a wondrous antiquity of the air (James *LT* 1993a: 198) when he sees Roman ruins. He is reminded of the passing greatness of the Monarchy by the ruins of Chambord (James *LT* 1993a: 57), and he associates classical houses with Revolutionary anger at Nantes. This method is used systematically by James to represent a sense of history in his book. As in Chambord, at Arles, the Roman ruins give a voice to the past: the arena is filled with the sounds of the circus (James *LT* 1993a: 216), and the theatre is full of delicate intonations and cadences (James *LT* 1993a: 217). At Blois Castle, the sixteenth-century closes around the viewer as "the expressive faces of an age in which human passions lay so near the surface seem to peep out at you from the windows, from the balconies, from the . . . sculpture" (James *LT* 1993a: 46). James thus comments on the meaning architecture carries for him: "this *transcendent piece of architecture* is the most joyous utterance of the French Renaissance" (James *LT* 1993a: 46, emphasis mine). James's picturesque scenes of French history provide impressions of historical facts, in which the visual input is provided by a building from the past. One could call it his "architectural method" of representing the past. The example of Nîmes offers revelations about the air of Gallo-Roman antiquity, as we have seen in the introduction, and the reports of James's happy excursions to Carcassonne and Chenonceaux illustrate his "architectural method" further by his evocations of the French Middle Ages and of the French Renaissance.

James spends felicitous hours at Carcassonne, filled with a great emotion the sentimental tourist wishes to share. The medieval castle stands alone on its hill, a fantastic array of fortifications (James *LT* 1993a: 161–2). Looking for an impression, he walks around the walls and imagines that the ruins before the restorations by M. Viollet-le-Duc were more affecting, but at first writes forgivingly: "as we see it today it is a wonderful evocation; and if there is a great deal of new in the old, there is plenty of old in the new" (James *LT* 1993a: 163). His later comments are more scathing, and eventually he declares: "I prefer in every case the ruined, however ruined, to the reconstructed, however splendid. What is left is more precious than what is added; one is history, the other is fiction; and I like the former the better of the two – it is so much more romantic" (James *LT* 1993a: 170).[5]

James calls Chenonceaux the architectural gem of Touraine. He knows that much has been written about it, but as a report seems obligatory, he sets out to convey his impressions (James *LT* 1993a: 68). The Renaissance façade and the attic impress him as some of the most "finished" (James *LT* 1993a: 70) in Touraine. He states that the place is neither a castle nor a palace, it is much rather a villa designed for a life of recreation. After describing the view of the palace from the gardens, James proceeds to tell the personal and sentimental history of the place: it was erected on the foundations of an old mill in 1515, became the property of Francis I, and his son Henry II gave it to Diana of Poitiers, his mistress. Upon the death of Henry II, his wife, Catherine de' Medici, turned Diana out of doors. Catherine built the wing of the castle that "carries itself across the river" (James *LT* 1993a: 71). As James reports about different owners, he imagines the life of the villa in its best years:

> The sixty years that preceded the Revolution were the golden age of fireside talk and of those amenities that proceed from the presence of women in whom the social art is both instinctive and acquired. The women of that period were, above all, good company; . . . Chenonceaux offered a perfect setting to free conversation; and infinite joyous discourse must have mingled with the liquid murmur of the Cher. . . . But I have wandered far from my story, which is simply a sketch of the surface of the place.
>
> (James *LT* 1993a: 72–3)

He goes on describing the rooms and the view, and finally he offers the picture of Chenonceaux that pleases him: from the other side of the Cher, in the evening light. In James's representation, the picturesque Renaissance villa is associated with the time of the French salons of the eighteenth century. No wonder that at the end of the day, enjoying a fine dinner at the little inn at Chenonceaux, the visitors "exchange remarks about the superior civilisation of France" (James *LT* 1993a: 74).

As part of his interest in architecture and history, James has an eye for tombs that record the memory of a person after death. He highlights two Renaissance tombs in particular, both ordered by Anne of Brittany: one at Tours for her two children (James *LT* 1993a: 28), and the other at Nantes for her parents (James *LT* 1993a: 123). The figures of both tombs are realistically portrayed. Renaissance artists believed, James writes, that the marble image "protected . . . the memory" (James *LT* 1993a: 123) of the dead person. By contrast, a modern tomb presents a scepticism in this regard, as he shows in his description of the tomb of general Lamorcière, defender of

Pope Pius IX, commemorated by a pedantic work from 1876 (James *LT* 1993a: 124). Even when he describes tombs, James offers glimpses of the life of a past era.

In his architectural descriptions of places, James suffuses his images by his sense of French history. Relying on his picturesque method, he uses architecture as the visual starting point for his illuminations about the past, which I have named the "architectural method." By using it, James exceeds the limits of his intended story, the sketch of the surface of places, and conveys his own sense of the historical and social relations of a past era, rich with beauty and blood, sweetness and suffering.

Senses of history in relation to national stereotypes (1884)

In *A Little Tour* the peculiar interest in history is accompanied by a wincing interest in the present. Naturally, most of the remarks involve the French and Frenchness, but characteristics of other nations, including England, the United States, and Italy, are also mentioned. The historical perspective resurfaces in these remarks, and his contemporary age is compared to previous ones as sceptical, technical, and commodity oriented.

In his Preface James writes he is sorry his formative relation to France and the French remains absent in *A Little Tour*. It seems to me, however, that the book gives away quite a few clues about his relation to France. As the most important point, it is made clear that James loves the French: he adores French women, makes fun of French men, admires French civilization, and offers humorous metaphors for Frenchness. As a key point of his attraction, he keeps noticing the activities of modern French women, who need to be counted with, as there is "no branch of human activity in which they are not involved" (James *LT* 1993a: 82). They not only hire vehicles, they also work at inns, as conductresses of tramcars (James *LT* 1993a: 174), or even as portresses (James *LT* 1993a: 100). At Arles, he admires a *dame de comptoire*, a handsome robust Arlésienne in her forties, who gives change at a café with the dignity of "a Roman empress" (James *LT* 1993a: 214).

On the other hand, French men provoke his sense for satire. The doorkeeper at Carcassonne keeps prattling on to display his knowledge. For James, the doorkeeper represents a typical Frenchman:

> a man of the people, . . . extremely intelligent, full of special knowledge and yet remaining of the people and showing his intelligence with a kind of ferocity, of defiance . . . a terrible pattern of a man, permeated in a high degree by civilisation yet untouched by the desire which

one finds in the Englishman in proportion as he rises in the world, to
approximate the figure of a gentleman.

(James *LT* 1993a: 168)

James is troubled to find the prototype of the self-reliant, democratic *cit-
oyen* of the Revolutionary streets in the guide's loud voice and volubility.
He also shudders at meeting an engineer-like monk (James *LT* 1993a: 142),
who reads "the 'Figaro'" seriously like an encyclical and whose answers
are precise and dry. James criticizes the appearance of French men as well:
he seldom meets a well-dressed French male, all come with muddy boots
and unshaven beards (James *LT* 1993a: 149). Their manners amend these
shortcomings though, as they are always excellent.

The French manners come from long years of tradition; they are an
acquired social art. James reveals his adoration for French civilization during his transcendental mood at Le Mans. Listening to French conversation,
he feels he is immersed in "a sense of the completeness of French life and
of the lightness and brightness of the social air, together with the desire
to arrive at friendly judgments, to express a positive interest" (James *LT*
1993a: 112). James remarks on French productivity, the "industry of the
wonderful country which produces, above all, the agreeable things of life,
and turns even its defeats and revolutions into gold" (James *LT* 1993a: 144).
He makes a joke of comparing the French mind to good claret at Bordeaux,
where he failed to find any good wine actually. He wishes to "pretend that
there is a taste of sound Bordeaux in the happiest manifestations of that
fine organ (the French mind), and that, correspondingly, there is a touch of
French reason, French completeness, in a glass of Pontet-Canet" (James
LT 1993a: 144) – yet he is unable to prove this analogy. Although there is
a huge wine exhibition going on at the town, among the many bottles on
show he finds not one he can taste. Moreover, considering that degustation
is a highly idiosyncratic act, there would be no verification but illumination
as a "result" of the analogy. The making of the French mind engages him at
Tours already, where he finds statues of Rabelais and Descartes but not of
Balzac, and comments that the two figures mark the two opposite poles to
which the wondrous French mind has travelled, the sensible and the meta-
physical, and half of Balzac's genius "looks in one direction and half in the
other" (James *LT* 1993a: 24). James admires the versatility and also the
unfathomable quality of the French mind.

Comparisons of Americans, English, and Italians frame James's comments about the French. At Bourges, a small café triggers a comparison
of generalizations about the French, the English, and the Americans (US).
A French café comes with a *materfamilias* who presides over the spot as
she sits under the mirror behind the *comptoir*, giving change, doling out

sugar, in this case even darning a stocking. The English public house or the commercial room serve for selling whiskey and smoking pipes and possess no homey feature. For James, French lads with cigarettes at cafés appear less brutal and heavy than English lads with their pipes at pubs (James *LT* 1993a: 106). The architectural image of the café appears a much more civilized spot than a pub or a saloon, James concludes. In a similar vein, cathedrals also provide a setting to start a comparison: a cathedral town in France can be dull, expressionless and ugly like Bourges (James *LT* 1993a: 104), but in Italy a cathedral city is always charming, while in England it can be sleepy but is surely "mellow." James introduces his generalizations connected to the sights he sees: as he loves gradations when he compares cathedrals (James *LT* 1993a: 122), so does he compare national characteristics.

However strong James's devotion to the French may be, Italian landscapes and architecture function as his supreme examples for the picturesque. He is reminded of the Italian side of the Alps as he goes South by gradations (James *LT* 1993a: 127), his love of the South is connected with his feelings for Italy. Excellent Pisan views and Siena brickwork come to his mind at Toulouse (James *LT* 1993a: 150, 158). He is aware of this "habit of constantly referring to the landscape of Italy as if that were the measure of the beauty of every other" (James *LT* 1993a: 148) and regards it the idle habit of an idle tourist, part of the sentimental project.

James's chatty reports on diverse senses of the past are complemented by isolated and sour comments on modern times. His visit to the Exhibition at Bordeaux is a good example. The show displays technological advancement and the mass production of wine; the boxes and pyramids of wine are meant for the eyes only, and not for individual consumption (James *LT* 1993a: 144). All articles on display are new, mass produced, smart – and for James, useless (James *LT* 1993a: 145). The only human element in the whole affair he notices are the Caribbean Indians on display,[6] who are not new, not smiling, but look "ancient, indifferent, terribly bored" (James *LT* 1993a: 146). This is the privileged spectator's direct look at the colonial native that is very rare in James, whose "aggressive" spectatorship is usually understood in terms of his grasping, all-determining imaginative vision (Rawlings 2009: 182). At Bourges, he is impressed by the house of Jacques Coeur, the "medieval capitalist" (James *LT* 1993a: 97): it is enormous and must have seemed vulgar at the time it was erected (James *LT* 1993a: 100). A comparative hint at Cornelius Vanderbilt's house (at Biltmore) recalls James's critical representation of its vast emptiness in *The American Scene* (Kovács 2014: 78–9; Luria 1997: 300).

As a summary of his attitude to modern times, the account of his visit to a faience artist's small factory and shop at Blois speaks volumes of what he dislikes in the present. "As we all know, this is an age of prose, of machinery, of wholesale production, of coarse and hasty processes" (James *LT* 1993a: 49), he writes. To this he prefers what he sees at the small factory: the shop looks like a parlor, the storeroom like a household, the salesman like a landlord; there is "the sense of a less eager activity and a greater search for perfection . . . without the smoke, the bustle, the ugliness of so much of our modern industry" (James *LT* 1993a: 49). It is easy to spot James's architectural method in this picture, in which the implied image of the modern factory functions as the trace of the modern era and the bustle of modern "industry" refers to both factory and general attitude.

On the basis of these remarks one can claim that the other tourist James professes not to write for in the Preface is the modern tourist, who is information oriented, practical, and interested in technical lore. In all the above asides an opposition is created between modern times and the past, and it is easy to make out from them a sense of nostalgia for times past that can be imagined through the architectural method. At the same time, the retrospective imagination "cannot afford to be foolish" and remain blind to the fact that there is no more possibility for political restauration than for cultural de-modernization of his time.

Conclusion

James's travel writing about France shows a particular concern with historical places, names, and events. However, this interest does not simply consist of learning facts about the past. James takes on the position of the sentimental tourist and he reconstructs data he chooses in the form of personal impressions of the past through his retrospective imagination. In *A Little Tour* James is seeking to produce a string of verbalized picturesque impressions of rural and small-town French scenes. These scenes illustrate a historical quality of "Frenchness" that usually escapes travellers who identify France with Paris. For James, mental pictures capture visual impressions of senses of the French past at specific locations. These locations are sometimes natural but mainly architectural. James is especially fond of representing non-restored ruins at the twilight hour that evoke a feeling and a sense of the past and also allow for the work of imaginative processing. This method of associating a building with the sense of the past was named James's "architectural method." James likes to reimagine three historical eras and their architectural traces in particular: the Gallo-Roman, the French Middle Ages, and the French Renaissance. He dislikes every trace of the French Revolution, which he usually captures in the form of what buildings it destroyed. The reason for this attitude is James's interest in French cultural continuity the Revolution disrupted. For James, the memory of French cultural continuity is most evident in visual culture, especially in architecture. The picturesque impressions of *A Little Tour* constitute emotionally touching, both happy and frightening, personal mental images in verbalized form that serve to create diverse impressions of senses of the French past for the traveller. The impressions of the past form a sharp contrast with James's impressions of his own technologically oriented faceless modern culture. The project of the sentimental tourist is to allow its readers picturesque glimpses of the continuity of French civilization which can prevail among uniformizing processes of modernization.

Notes

1 *A Little Tour* could be compared to *The American* or *The Ambassadors* because of the similar rural French scenes, but it could also be read along with *Italian Hours* because of the similarity of perspective and evaluation, or with *The American Scene* because of comparable themes: the South, the past, and the role of buildings.

2 James described his strategies of the creative process in his essays as sensual data through imaginative reprocessing verbalized in a narrative perspective that gives the scene new, morally motivated, meanings, see Ágnes Zsófia Kovács (2006), *The Function of the Imagination in the Writings of Henry James: The Production of a Civilized Experience*, Lewiston: Mellen: 213–14.

3 The connection between historical continuity and architectural traditions is pointed out in Edith Wharton's travel pieces on France as well. In 1908, Wharton published *A Motor Flight through France,* where she explained and showed the work of French historical continuity in elements of the built environment in small-town France. Wharton had definitely read James on France, actually travelled with him in rural France in her motor car, and eventually produced her own narrative version of French continuity in 1908. Then, in 1915, Wharton published her *Fighting France*, a string of reports on her visits to the front lines in France at the beginning of the Great War. These accounts report the threat to French historical continuity the war brings, especially through minute visual representations of ruined architecture. So in the wartime, Wharton went on using her architectural language of continuity, but instead of celebrating sights, her tone became concerned and sometimes alarming, a feature that later earned her piece the name "war propaganda." For details see Ágnes Zsófia Kovács, "Edith Wharton's Vision of Continuity in Wartime France," *Neohelicon*, vol. 44, no. 2, 545–58. DOI:10.1007/s11059-017-0391-z.

4 James relates to the ideas of the Paterian Aesthetic Movement ambivalently, with criticism and engagement at the same time, see Aladár Sarbu (2010), "The Lure of Lacedaemon: A Note on Pater and Modernism," *Publicationes Universitatis Miskolciensis*, vol. 15, no. 2: 71.

5 In his picturesque scenes of the past, James prefers to present architectural ruins than fully renovated buildings and always asserts his dislike for renovations. He finds Marmontier "edited" (James *LT* 1993a: 38), vulgar and mechanical (39). At Blois the restorations of Renaissance chateau chills the imagination (42, 43), it is overdone, too colorful, too fresh (47). At Angers the restoration seems disagreeable, the place has been done up (114). The only good restoration he mentions is at Amboise, where excrescence is being removed (61). Carcassonne itself looks

too perfect (160), as it has been converted from an irresponsible old town into a conscious museum specimen (162). In contrast, Aigues-Mortes has not been renovated and it impresses James as miraculous (194).

6 Bordeaux was the second biggest port and ship-manufacturing city after Marseille, the centre for the trade with the French colonies in the Caribbean from the seventeenth century on (Ziéglé and Garrigou 1998: 17–18).

Bibliography

Benert, Annette Larson (1996) "Edith Wharton at War: Civilized Space in Troubled Times," *Twentieth Century Literature*, vol. 42, no. 3: 322–43.

Bradbury, Nicola (2004) "'While I waggled my small feet': Henry James's Return to Paris," *The Yearbook of English Studies*, vol. 34: 186–93.

Buelens, Gert, ed. (1997) *Enacting History in Henry James*, Cambridge: Cambridge University Press.

Buitenhuis, Peter (1957) "Aesthetics of the Skyscraper: The Views of Sullivan, James and Wright," *American Quarterly*, vol. 9, no. 3: 316–24.

Buzard, James (1993) *The Beaten Track: European Tourism, Literature, and the Ways of Culture, 1800–1918*. Oxford: Clarendon.

Follini, Tamara L. (2014) "Speaking Monuments: Henry James, Walt Whitman, and the Civil War Statues of Augustus Saint-Gaudens," *Journal of American Studies*, vol. 48, no. 1: 25–49.

Haralson, Eric and Kendall Johnson (2009) *Critical Companion to Henry James: A Literary Reference to his Life and Work*, New York: Facts on File, Infobase Publishing.

Herford, Oliver (2016) *Henry James's Style of Retrospect: Late Personal Writings*, 1890–1915, Oxford: Oxford University Press.

Horne, Philip (1990) *Henry James and Revision*, Oxford: Clarendon.

Howard, Richard (1993) "Note on the Texts," *Collected Travel Writings: The Continent* by Henry James, edited by Richard Howard, New York: Library of America: 792–6.

James, Henry (1993a) *Collected Travel Writings: The Continent*, edited by Richard Howard, New York: Library of America.

——— (1993b) *The American Scene, Collected Travel Writings: Great Britain and America*, edited by Henry James and Richard Howard, New York: Library of America: 351–736.

——— (1993c) *Collected Travel Writings: Great Britain and America*, edited by Richard Howard, New York: Library of America.

——— (1993d) *Italian Hours, Collected Travel Writings: The Continent*, edited by Henry James and Richard Howard, New York: Library of America: 279–620.

——— (1993e) *A Little Tour in France, Collected Travel Writings: The Continent*, edited by Henry James and Richard Howard, New York: Library of America: 1–278.

Kermode, Frank (1999) "Attracting, Taking, Holding: Tony Tanner and Henry James," *Critical Quarterly*, vol. 41, no. 2: 60–2.

Kovács, Ágnes Zsófia (2006) *The Function of the Imagination in the Writings of Henry James: The Production of a Civilized Experience*, Lewiston, NY: The Mellen Press.

———— (2014) "James's Sense of American Civil War in *The American Scene*," *Henry James Goes to War*, edited by Miroslawa Buchholtz et al., Frankfurt: Peter Lang: 75–90.

———— (2017) "Edith Wharton's Vision of Continuity in Wartime France," *Neohelicon*, vol. 44, no. 2: 541–62.

Luria, Sarah (1997) "The Architecture of Manners: Henry James, Edith Wharton, and the Mount," *American Quarterly*, vol. 49, no. 2: 298–327.

McWhirter, David (1997) " 'A provision full of responsibilities': Senses of the Past in Henry James' Fourth Phase," *Enacting History in Henry James*, edited by Gert Buelens. Cambridge: Cambridge University Press: 148–65.

Rawlings, Peter (2004) "Grotesque Encounters in the Travel Writing by Henry James," *Yearbook of English Studies*, vol. 34: 171–85.

———— (2009) "James and the Swelling Act of the Imperial Theme," *American Travel and Empire*, edited by Susan Castillo and David Seed, Liverpool: Liverpool University Press: 174–99.

Sarbu, Aladár (2010) "The Lure of Lacedaemon: A Note on Pater and Modernism," *Publicationes Universitatis Miskolciensis*, vol. 15, no. 2: 71–85.

Sterne, Laurence (1768) *A Sentimental Journey to France and Italy by Mr. Yorick*, vol. 1, London: T. Becket and P. A. De Hondt.

Sterne, Laurence (1774) *A Sentimental Journey to France and Italy by Mr. Yorick*, vol. 1, London: P. Miller and J. White.

Stowe, William W. (1994) *Going Abroad: European Travel in Nineteenth-Century American Culture*, Princeton, NJ: Princeton University Press.

Tanner, Tony (1995) *Henry James and the Art of Nonfiction*, Athens: Georgia University Press.

Ziéglé, Anne and Agnès Garrigou (1998) "Bordeaux, Port de la façade Atlantique et ses relations commercialies avecles Indies orientales," *La Route des Indes: Les Indes et l'Europe: échanges artistiques et heritage commun, 1650–1850*, edited by Henry-Claude Cousseau, Paris: Somogy Éditions & Bordeaux: Musée d'Aquitaine: 17–25.

3 Self-inscription and autoethnography in Henry James's travel writing

Selma Mokrani

Henry James was taught from his tender age that "in Europe . . . there was Art" and that Europe could provide "some finer kind of social issue" (James *Letters*, vol. 1 1974: 160). As a young man, he embarked on the Grand Tour to crown the record of his formal education. His subsequent travels were meant for further cultural acquisition and for full-grown revision of earlier impressions. After a permanent residence in England, he undertook the most remarkable "voyage" of his later phase – his homecoming trip to America, to which he poignantly testified in *The American Scene*.

Travel provided James with a shrewd intellectual outlook which allowed him to institute his personal and professional mastery, embolden his perception, boost his creative powers, and store his impressions for fictional deployment. For him, travel is not only a cultural practice of movement but also a consolidation of authority. In this chapter, I attempt to explore different modes of James's self-inscription in *A Little Tour in France* (1900)[1] and *Italian Hours* (1909).[2] I also suggest that such modes culminate in autoethnography in *The American Scene* (1907). James's self-inscription allows him to assume authority, showcasing the continuity between his experience of selfhood and his authority as an empirical witness, often driven by the "ethnographic impulse."[3] I explore James's immersion in his travel narratives as a character, interacting with an experiential repertory rather than with actual humans. I try to demonstrate James's placement of himself within traditions of travel writing, consolidating his authority by circumventing the overwhelming control of John Ruskin and by invalidating the "defenseless" aspirations of George Eliot. Finally, I illustrate the autoethnographic turn in *The American Scene* with focus on James's diegetic status, as well as embodiment and reciprocity, which transform him from a "recalcitrant" to a "vulnerable" observer.

Travel writing is characterized by chronotopicity[4] since its temporal and spatial markers are indivisible. Yet, in most cases, the moment of travelling is different from that of writing, which unavoidably gives way to special protocols of representation. Glenn Hooper and Tim Youngs link journey to narrative, arguing that the former's fluidity determines the latter's indefiniteness and generic adaptability: "In much the same way that travel itself can be seen as a somewhat fluid experience, so too can travel writing be regarded as a relatively open-ended and versatile form" (2004: 3).[5] Despite the fact that travel's multidirectional spatiality is sometimes liable to render it non-narrative, travel writing possesses an intrinsic narrative potential by virtue of its constitutive temporal and spatial structures.[6]

Since James often embarks on journeys as a precondition for writing, he enlists to Michel Butor's famous assertion: "I travel in order to write" (2001: 69). His travel accounts are packaged either as proper literary travelogues and guidebooks or as private journals, diaries, notes, and letters home from abroad. Most commonly, James's records of travel are reconstructed, processed, and written up following the chronology of the movement of travel itself. Therefore, his task overpasses that of compilation to that of reinvention through the dual pattern of journey and narrative. This process ultimately involves assortments and erasures. Moreover, his texts depend on the stimulation of an experiential stock, becoming thus ideal grounds for intertextuality and confirming the fact that fictional travel naturally impinges on actual travel.

Experiential repertories,[7] intertextuality, and fictionalization

James's experiential repertories render his travel writing persistently intertextual. *A Little Tour in France* abounds in examples of literary, artistic, and historical confluences. At Tours, James tries hard to spot the house of Mademoiselle Gamard, "the sinister old maid" of Balzac's *Le Curé de Tours* (James *LT* 1900: 12) as well as that of Tristan l'Hermite, the provost-marshal in Walter Scott's historical novel *Quentin Durward* (James *LT* 1900: 24). His motivation to visit places is mainly prompted by their connection to literary figures and fictional characters. He expresses his disappointment when at Bourges "I saw no one who reminded me of Balzac's 'illustre Gaudissart'" (James *LT* 1900: 100).

On the other hand, despite his fascination with a faience artist at Blois, James refrains from conveying the interesting exchange they had about pottery (James *LT* 1900: 42), and later blames the surprising lack of human interaction around a *table d'hôte* on "the change that had . . . come over the spirit of the people" (James *LT* 1900: 100). In addition, he evokes absolute authorial hegemony and the ensuing absence of counterpoint when he lengthily describes the "learned," "sociable" employee at the prefecture, who "will never read these pages" (James *LT* 1900: 197). Similarly, he reflects on his eminent privilege with regard to the doorkeeper of the citadel at Carcassonne, to whose description he devotes over three pages, but "who can know nothing of the liberties I am taking with him" (James *LT* 1900: 203).

James produced travelogues that generally fused the aesthetic and ideological purposes of the travel book with the practical function of the guidebook.[8] He, for example, travelled to France "to do [the] specific chore" (qtd. in Edel 1985: 282) of writing *A Little Tour in France*. His target was to produce a guidebook in the strictest sense.[9] Leon Edel noted that "[t]he account he wrote of his little tour is much less personal than his other travel writings [and] much more strictly a guidebook" (1985: 282). However, as the following discussion will demonstrate, this book surpasses by far the conventions of the mere guidebook.

In the vein of the guidebook, *A Little Tour in France* scrupulously provides historical details of Old Gaul and the Renaissance. James enumerates important monuments and edifices, offers extensive details on the stories of monarchs and dukes, quotes different French historians' comments on the record of remarkable buildings and goes to great lengths to present the history associated with the names of old French houses. Yet, while doing all these things, he goes beyond the mere reporting of historical facts to reconstitute the reality, restore lost memories, and piece up the lost fragments of history together through the work of his imagination. In short, as he himself confesses, he "undertakes a little restoration of his own" (James *LT* 1900: 40).

Intertextuality is manifest in the recurring references to historical sources in order to convey veracity and to emphasize reliability. James predicates his authority on historical sources and guidebooks which he commends without reserve. He substantiates his descriptions with information from *Murray*, which he describes as "my faithful Murray" (James *LT* 1900: 226), and the *Guide Joanne*,[10] which he qualifies as "excellent" (James *LT* 1900: 89). He also refers to history books such as Pierre Clément's *Jacques Cœur et Charles VII, ou la France au quinzième siècle, étude historique* (1853).

It is also possible to argue that intertextuality is tightly linked to fictionalization. Both involve characterization which, in turn, engages associations with textual and socio-historical paradigms. James's characterization is either metonymical or metaphorical. The former rests on the representational dimension; the latter dwells on textual and extra-textual correspondences. As an example of metonymical characterization, the nun at Marmoutier, with "pointed features, an intensely distinct enunciation, and . . . pretty manners," so accurately duplicates the "teachings" that the Catholic Church "instills into its functionaries" (James *LT* 1900: 27).

Metaphorical characterization is illustrated by James's highlighting of the textual trope of character. The gentleman he encounters on the road to Nîmes "might have stepped out of a novel of Octave Feuillet" (James *LT* 1900: 228), and an old priest and a monk on the train to Angoulême look "almost as vivid as the actors in the *Comédie Humaine*" (James *LT* 1900: 168). James's imagination ventures towards the consummation of a Balzacian scene by narrativizing this chance encounter. He starts guessing at the old priest's life-experience, concluding that he must have "seen a good deal both of the church and of the world." He also surmises about his "extraordinary bag, which . . . appeared to contain the odds and ends of a lifetime" (James *LT* 1900: 168). James even writes his own self as a character, not only in his own travel account, but also in the real-life replica of Balzac's *Comédie Humaine*. Were it not for the forbidding, "reserved" monk, James would have "enter[ed] into conversation" with the "delightful old priest" (James *LT* 1900: 168).

Metaphorical characterization also involves intertextual allusions to socio-historical cases in the rendition of a possible version of a person. In *Italian Hours*, a passing young man who is part of the "operatic" scene of an old picturesque city in Genoa answers all of James's romantic expectations and represents to him "a graceful ornament to the prospect" of fictionalization (James *IH* 1909: 117). However, after a brief conversation with the young man, James's fabula is arrested by the stark truth that this "harmonious little figure in the middle distance" is but a radical communist, an antiroyalist, and an anarchist. After having built a speculative narrative on the stranger's identity, character, and life, James is brought back to reality by realizing that he "was an unhappy, underfed, unemployed young man, who took a hard, grim view of everything and was operatic only quite in spite of himself" (James *IH* 1909: 117).

Jean Viviès affirms that the travel account is definitely a "montage" because it is located "at the meeting point – or the point of contradiction – between sight and insight, between inventory and invention and between fragment and whole" (2002: 107). James's montage basically involves the rehabilitation of amorphous notes taken on the spot. Diaries, journals, and photographs[11] serve him as *aide-mémoire*. In his preface to *A Little Tour in France*, he explains that given the passage of time and the "dismal work" caused by "interruptions," travel writing becomes an "indirect tribute" (James *LT* 1900: vi). Recollection is therefore a pivotal mechanism of James's travel writing. It involves the retrieval of the sense of immediacy from the past act of witnessing and the critical reflection on the lesson of the journey. His journey's itineraries are not predetermined but reestablished through retrospection. Hence, his task is not simply to put into words the elements of the fulfilled journey but squarely to *reinvent* the journey.

Viviès interestingly points to the repetitive pattern of travel writing: "Narrating the voyage amounts to playing the pattern out a second time," giving the travel narrative a "double configuration"; it is more a "discourse that subsumes both the journey and its narration" (2002: 110). To James, such "double configuration" is expedient for self-inscription. Quite precociously, he employs the postmodern technique of *mise en abyme* to mirror the process of composition, making some of his passages diegetically self-conscious. James reminds his readers that he is actually *quoting* from his notebook. He reports that the Château d'Angers is " 'Stupidly and vulgarly modernized' – that is another flower from my note-book, and note-books are not obliged to be reasonable. 'There are some narrow and tortuous streets, with a few curious old houses,' I continue to quote" (James *LT* 1900: 131). Later, he evokes the Maison d'Adam in Angers, stating that "A little reflection now convinces me that such a form is a distinction; and, indeed, I find it mentioned, rather inconsistently, in my note-book, a little further on, as 'extremely simple and grand'" (James *LT* 1900: 134). Through such mirroring, James challenges the passivity of merely replaying the pattern a second time. Self-conscious references to the process of composition enable him to reconnect with his old self as a direct note-taking witness. More significantly, by soliciting his notebook, he further affirms his authority by asserting his veritable chronotopic presence.

James considers the travel writer "a collector of memories" and a later consumer of impressions in more single-minded states of mind (James *IH* 1909: 12). Hence, since Venice is too captivating to be "a place for concentration of mind" (James *IH* 1909: 13), the moments spent in the midst of its exquisite beauty "should be devoted to collecting impressions"; while "[a]fterwards, in ugly places, at unprivileged times, you can convert your impressions into prose" (James *IH* 1909: 14). Recognizing that the whole work of travel writing is a work of memory, James, who is governed by "fond reminiscence," calls himself "an undiscourageable gatherer of the sense of things" (James *IH* 1909: 261, 267).

Interestingly, James highlights the intensity of aesthetic emotion on memory.[12] To him, it is the "freshness of a great emotion" (James *LT* 1900: 191) that is able to reclaim old memories of places and people. The interplay between mood, feeling, and memory is capable of activating selective information and of mobilizing a certain ordering of events which narrativizes his travel accounts. As a traveller he experiences "melancholy moments," "disappointments," as well as "satisfactions." Therefore, "the rounded felicity" he senses while writing up his account is capable of repairing clefts and of filling voids (James *LT* 1900: 191).

James admits that he does engage in protraction in the process of writing. He, for instance, attributes the difficulty of doing justice to the historic cities of Italy to the fact that he has "to draw upon recollections now three years old," which compels him to seek imaginative compensation in order "to make my short story a long one" (James *IH* 1909: 53). Moreover, he admits that any record of travel presents the writer with a paradox, even guilt, lest he should take a certain "liberty" with it: "There are considerations, proprieties, a necessary indirectness," which impose themselves and make the writer use "a little art" (James *IH* 1909: 64). There is indeed no escape from the exercise of "a little art" because "[o]ne sees, after all . . . even among the most palpable realities . . . the play of one's imagination" (James *IH* 1909: 149).

"The Ruskinian contagion" and the belated "charmed *flâneur*"

Michel Butor underscores the triad of travel, reading, and writing in which "bookish voyages" with a "library of travel" are crucial to travellers who often read authoritative sources by forerunners to substantiate their travel accounts (2001: 83). "Anxiety of influence," "belatedness" or "secondariness,"[13] and the question of literary appropriation play a major role in the construction of authorial subjectivity. They encroach upon the composition processes and illustrate the travel writer's restless quest for originality. James so ably sums up the difficulty of such a quest when he admits with frustration that Venice, "the vast museum," is unwilling to yield an "original" view to the "sentimental tourist" who "likes to be alone; to be original; to have (to himself, at least) the air of making discoveries." Unfortunately, "[t]here is nothing left to discover or describe, and originality of attitude is completely impossible" (James *IH* 1909: 5). John Ruskin, an authority in Italian travel, is one of the most eminent causes of unattainable originality. His masterful influence placed him in a symbolical position of surveillance over subsequent travellers and travel writers. James admits that he actually seeks "a pusillanimous safety in the trivial and the obvious" because he strongly feels "the eye of Mr. Ruskin . . . upon us; [therefore] we grow nervous and lose our confidence" (James *IH* 1909: 43). Nonetheless, James strives to disengage his imaginative space from his predecessor's impressions. He had purchased Ruskin's *Mornings in Florence* and *Stones of Venice* and had read passages aloud to his travelling companions, but he would later regret having bought these books and would even call them "invidious and insane" (James *IH* 1909: 128).

But the fact that James devotes lengthy and ubiquitous passages to the discussion of Ruskin in *Italian Hours* attests to his "anguish of contamination."[14] James proceeds by creating a dialogue with Ruskin, quoting his statements and replying instantly. Ruskin had given a bleak picture of the city of Venice with reference to the events of the Risorgimento. James exonerates himself from this outlook by declaring that "[f]ortunately one reacts against the *Ruskinian contagion*, and one hour of the lagoon is worth a hundred pages of demoralized prose" (James *IH* 1909: 2, emphasis added). After reading *Mornings in Florence*, James finds fault with Ruskin's caution to Italian people to be "artistic"; he believes that this admonition is haughty and ungrateful to a people with such a rich artistic heritage (James *IH* 1909: 126). Although James shares Ruskin's rebuttal of "modern profanation" (James *IH* 1909: 129), he sees that Ruskin's lamentation over the loss of old Florentine ways, especially as manifested in the cab-stand at the foot of Giotto's Tower, is an indication of his "ill-humour" (James *IH* 1909: 126).

James also realizes that Ruskin overstates the artistic lacunas of Florentine monuments and pictures. While haunted with the feeling that he is a poor judge of art in comparison to Ruskin, James judges his predecessor's admonitions as "dry and pedantic," even comically "pedagogic." He finally "los[es] patience" with Ruskin and wonders "by what right this informal votary of form pretended to run riot through a poor charmed *flâneur*'s quiet contemplations, his attachment to the noblest of pleasures, his enjoyment of the loveliest of cities" (James *IH* 1909: 128). James concludes that Ruskin's prescriptive method is irrelevant to an Italian context where "art [is] spontaneous, joyous, irresponsible" (James *IH* 1909: 129), and depends on the artist's "representational impulse" (James *IH* 1909: 129).

In *A Little Tour in France*, James assumes a corrective stance, short of the sense of belatedness. Rousseau's description in his *Confessions* of the château de Chenonceaux, "one of the most romantic houses in France" (James *LT* 1900: 69) is frustrating. He declares that his intention as a "later son of time" is to supersede that of Rousseau by paying "some larger tribute" to this edifice (James *LT* 1900: 70). On the other hand, he criticizes Stendhal's approach in *Mémoires d'un Touriste* for "want of appreciation of the picturesque." He differentiates his purpose from that of Stendhal's tourism-driven and commercial purpose, which gives attention to the "superficial aspects of things" (James *LT* 1900: 220). Furthermore, James even tries to prove Lamartine's descriptions of his own birthplace wrong. The house is after all not so vast but meager and shabby (James *LT* 1900: 326).

Penelope *sedente* and the cosmopolitan

Travel writing has been studied as the site of "recovery of the complex subject-positions of both men and women travellers" (Duncan and Gregory 1999: 3). More specifically, such approaches seek to determine how travel writing could be considered a sphere of women's self-knowledge and knowledge of the world. Mary Suzanne Schriber, for example, has addressed the problematic nature of imagining "self as writer" for women, especially as they have constantly been perceived as not more than "'idealizing appreciators'" (1997: 171). While formally denied to women, the Grand Tour was an institutionalized structure, "an ideological exercise," and "a social ritual," the purpose of which was to conclude the education of privileged young men "by exposing them to the treasured artifacts and ennobling society of the continent" (Buzard 2002: 38). James used his experiences as a "citizen of the world" as a winning card to assert his authority in comparison to George Eliot, who was more likely to be attached to the figure of a Penelope *sedente*.

In his review of John Walter Cross's biography of Eliot, titled "The Life of George Eliot" (1885),[15] James insists on the necessity of overlooking Eliot's limitations, reminding himself and her readers that she ought to be understood in the light of her own premises and with the consideration that her literary options were limited by her sedentariness. He attributes to Eliot qualifiers which suggest limitation and parochialism, remarking that her imagination enabled her "to sit at home with book and pen, and yet enter into the life of other generations" (James LGE 1970: 57–8). He ultimately presents her as the "home-keeping Mrs. Lewes" (James LGE 1970: 39), who was but a "sedentary, serious, invalidical English lady . . . without adventures or sensations" (James LGE 1970: 61).

James also insists on defining Eliot's sources of knowledge as deskbound. He believes that *Romola*, a historical novel set in fifteenth-century Italy, bears "to a maximum the in-door quality" (James LGE 1970: 56); it is "overladen with learning" and "smells of the lamp" (James LGE 1970: 55). Her description of Florentine life is to James an indication of homebound scholarship rather than immediate observation. Thus, her travels in Italy have failed to reverberate through her novel because she "proceeded by reflection and research" in her reconstruction of the remote past (James LGE 1970: 56).

Although James considers Eliot's union with Lewes "one of the most successful partnerships . . . in the history of human affection" (James LGE 1970: 47), he concurrently remarks that Eliot's "false position" generated an "effect of sequestration," which led her to develop "a kind of compensatory earnestness," necessarily assigning her to a monotonous life where there was no place for "the accidental" nor "the unexpected" (James LGE 1970: 46).

Interestingly, James is one of the first readers, and perhaps *the* first critic, of Eliot's travel journals which were first published as part of Cross's biography. They constitute part of the reviewed material he included in his essay "The Life of George Eliot." It is easy to guess that what has given ammunition to James in his criticism of Eliot is her negative response to Italy as her own journals testify. The first thing she remarks about Rome, for example, is that "there was nothing imposing to be seen." She even mistakes a Roman aqueduct for the ruins of baths (Eliot "Recollections of Italy" 1998a: 341). She also complains of "the heavy load of disappointment" and "the weary length of the [narrow and ugly] streets" leading to an unimpressive dome of St. Peter's cathedral and to the Castle of St. Angelo which were but "a shabby likeness of the engravings." She concludes that "[n]ot one iota had I seen that corresponded with my preconceptions," and expresses sorrow for parting with her sublime idea of a "Rome unvisited" (Eliot "Recollections of Italy" 1998a: 341). Likewise, the Baths of Titus in the Campagna are to her "damp and gloomy spaces"; the columns of the Forum have a "dreary effect" on her mind (Eliot "Recollections of Italy" 1998a: 343), and "the ugly, painful towers of Bologna" made her wish not to see them again (Eliot "Recollections of Italy" 1998a: 361). The closest she could come to ela- tion is her description of a sunset scene on the lagoon in a gondola, which made her "forget [her] own existence and feel melted into the general life" (Eliot "Recollections of Italy" 1998a: 365); and the closest she could come to emotional involvement is her remark on the graves of Keats and Shelley which were "unshaded by wall or trees." Looking at Keats's tomb deeply moved her "because of the inscription on the stone which seems to make him still speak in bitterness from his grave" (Eliot "Recollections of Italy" 1998a: 349).

In her account, Eliot shows disdain for time-worn and dusky paintings like Tintoretto's *Gloria del Paradisio* that James particularly values, and prefers paintings like *The Apotheosis of Venice* "which looks as fresh as if it were painted yesterday" (Eliot "Recollections of Italy" 1998a: 363). James, in contrast, prefers the old, faded, and pale mosaics to the shining, renewed surfaces (James *IH* 1909: 7). *In A Little Tour in France*, he justifies this predilection:

> For myself, I have no hesitation; I prefer in every case the ruined, how- ever ruined, to the reconstructed, however splendid. What is left is more precious than what is added: the one is history, the other is fiction; and I like the former the better of the two, – it is so much more romantic. One is positive, so far as it goes; the other fills up the void with things more dead than the void itself, inasmuch as they have never had life.
>
> (James *LT* 1900: 205)

Furthermore, James argues that Eliot has restricted her capacity for "pleas- ure . . . in the fact of representation for itself." Such a limitation, James opines, made her travel notes and journals "singularly vague in expression on the subject of the general and particular spectacle – the life and man- ners, the works of art." Despite all these drawbacks, James observes, such writings are rich in "the tempered enjoyment of foreign sights which was as near as she ever came to rapture" (James LGE 1970: 54). What James mostly reproaches her for is her emotionless inventory of the pictures and statues – a fault that bespeaks her "intellectual habits." He is especially provoked by an unaffected remark Eliot made on Michelangelo's celebrated sculptures on the tombs of the San Lorenzo Chapel in Florence. He bitterly quotes her statement that the sculptures "remained to us as affected and exaggerated in the original as in the copies and casts." James considers this declaration highly compromising to Eliot's artistic reputation and wryly speculates on Cross's unreserved publication of such material (James LGE 1970: 54).

After his first meeting with Eliot, James concluded that "she has a larger circumference than any woman I have ever seen" (James *LHJ*, vol. 1 1920: 117). His use of the word "circumference" unmistakably points to his thinking in terms of boundaries, namely, those of the male tradition. At the same time, he considerately tries to account for her scientific mindset. While underscoring her heavy reliance on "scientific observation," he explains that it is the ultimate result of "the contagion of [Lewes's] studies" (James LGE 1970: 52) – a contagion that yielded a total dependence on "reflection" at the expense of "emotion" (James LGE 1970: 53). James is right in making this connection: it is true that Eliot uses concepts from science and natural history in her novels and travel accounts. In her "Ilfracombe Journal," she deploys an impressive repertoire of marine zoology and specialized Latin nomenclature, which suggest authority and seriousness in research. This procedure is in itself transgressive because women at the time were "largely excluded from the institutional study of science" (Bellanca 1997: 21). Moreover, James's theory of the Lewes contamination is also true inasmuch as it exceeds mere influence. Being overwhelmed by Lewes's scholarly research, Eliot herself expressed anxiety at her idleness and qualified the "Ilfracombe Journal" as a "trifle" (Eliot 1998b: 62). Her appropriation of scientific vocabulary is therefore not simply a matter of influence but also an attempt to give some weightiness to her memoir, lest she should appear amateurish in contrast to her companion's professionalism.

Unlike Eliot, James has nothing to prove and is confident that his sentimentalism alone will pay off. He deliberately shuns away from assuming a guise of connoisseurship in his assessment of art objects. Throughout his travel writings, his comments on the paintings of the great masters are filled with a sense of awe and admiration and mostly show modesty as to his own powers of distinction. He for instance refrains from passing scientific judgement on the restoration work done on the outer walls of St. Mark's in Venice. Rather, he prefers to qualify himself as a "sentimental traveller" (James *IH* 1909: 205) who has no pretense to scientific and technical judgement: "We do not profess, however, to undertake a scientific quarrel with these changes; we admit that our complaint is a purely sentimental one" (James *IH* 1909: 9). If James's sentimentalism was crucial to his attempts to ensconce his authority as a contented foreigner, it was also, quite paradoxically, unsettling to his privilege as a yearning native.

The American Scene as autoethnography

Since travel writing is "generically elusive" (Holland and Huggan 2000: 12), and since it is located "as a practice that writes across generic boundaries, whether those of memoir or essay, journalism or pastoral, fiction or ethnography" (Caesar 1995: 115), the generic horizon of *The American Scene* could be expanded to include autoethnography. Autoethnography is itself "a blurred genre" which resists classification (Holman-Jones 2000: 756). *The American Scene* is also generically hard to pin down; it quite interestingly fits the description of autoethnography as located in "an intermediate space we can't quite define yet, a borderland between passion and intellect, analysis and subjectivity, ethnography and autobiography, art and life" (Behar 1996: 174). Furthermore, *The American Scene* can be considered an autoethnography in so far as it is evocative and dialogic, showcasing the mutuality between knowledge and feeling, self and other. Despite its scenic vocation, it still makes allowance for introspection and embodiment.

   The American Scene has mostly been read as "the eccentric travelogue of a reactionary aesthete" (Posnock 1991: vii). Ethnography has conventionally been part of a number of studies on travel.[16] Quite surprisingly, autoethnography has never been studied within the field of travel writing, and much less, within James scholarship. This seems all the more inexplicable since autoethnography has been defined as containing "tenets of autobiography and ethnography" (Ellis et al. 2011: 1), which are both important constituents of travel writing.

   Nancy Bentley has studied James's ethnographic interest as mainly reflected in his consistent interest in manners. She suggests that James uses a vocabulary of "totemic kinship" "when he describes Philadelphia society as the product of a 'scheme of consanguinity' that produces 'security'" (Bentley 1995: 117). Gert Buelens, on his part, suggests that in the Philadelphia Chapter of *The American Scene*, James "like an ethnographer . . . registers the ethos of a particular place from a secure perspective that is rooted in his own sense of character and propriety" (1999: 361). Both studies, therefore, remain within the insular framework of American high culture.

   Deborah Reed-Danahay's definition of autoethnography brings forth the association of autoethnography, ethnography, and autobiography. Her definition conforms to James's text in many different ways as the ensuing analysis will demonstrate. Reed-Danahay claims that "[t]he concept of autoethnography . . . synthesizes both a postmodern ethnography, in which the realist conventions and objective observer position of standard ethnography have been called into question, and a postmodern autobiography, in which the notion of the coherent, individual self has been similarly called into question" (1997: 2).

The American Scene is an autoethnographic text which, through inner voice and authentic response, approaches the fundamental issues of self and culture. While being a self-account of James's personal experience of repatriation, it stands out as a narrative of cultural identity. It is expressed through a powerfully affective way of perception in which the embodied researcher is himself the medium of inquiry.[17] It connects self and culture in its preoccupation with identity, authenticity, and voice. James's text is about personal and cultural self-identification, especially with regard to racial others. When he urgently starts negotiating his identity between confrontation and accommodation, he is transformed from a "recalcitrant observer" to a "vulnerable observer." His journey is staged in dramatic tension, leading to an epiphany about what it means to be an American.

James poses a crucial question springing from what Arthur Bochner calls "ethical self-consciousness" (2016: 213): "Which is the American, by these scant measures? – which is *not* the alien, over a large part of the country at least, and where does one put a finger on the dividing line, or, for that matter, 'spot' and identify any particular phase of the conversion. . .?" (James *AS* 1994: 95). James here shakes off the pretense of subjective wholeness. He goes on with another critical question which envelops a disclaimer of the term alien: "Who and what is an alien, when it comes to that, in a country peopled from the first under the jealous eye of history? – peopled, that is, by migrations at once extremely recent, perfectly traceable and urgently required" (James *AS* 1994: 95). Interestingly, James not only unsettles boundaries between self and other but also enables the silenced voices to speak back through the reciprocity and dialogism he creates with the alien. Such self-interrogations, followed by conclusive answers, dismantle his covetable status as a univocal inquirer and obliquely give counterpoint to the silent alien. Through such answered questionings, James achieves the status of the interlocutor[18] and secures narrative closure.

James's discomfort with regard to the "aliens" recalls Freud's notion of the uncanny which Julia Kristeva advocates as a strategy of cohabitation with "strangers." This notion stems from the comforting realization that the self is innately shifty and fragmented, and therefore open to "welcome[ing] strangers to that uncanny strangeness, which is as much theirs as it is ours" (Kristeva 1991: 191–2). The stranger is in Kristeva's words "the hidden face of our identity," and "[b]y recognizing him within ourselves, we are spared detesting him in himself" (1991: 1). Kristeva presses her point more assertively by negating the oddity of strangeness: "The foreigner comes in when the consciousness of my difference arises, and he disappears when we all acknowledge ourselves as foreigners, unamenable to bonds and communities" (1991: 1). This is precisely what James does throughout *The American Scene*.

In Italy and France, James had kept a critical distance generated by the freshness of being totally foreign, while in America he struggled with the liminal status of the native-turned-foreigner. He himself expresses his ambivalent position as both an insider and an outsider when he qualifies himself as at once "the initiated native" and "the enquiring stranger." His self-addressed epithets of "restored absentee," "reinstated absentee" (James *AS* 1994: 266), "repatriated absentee" (James *AS* 1994: 281), and "the subject long-expatriated" (James *AS* 1994: 224), point to a recognition that, in Kristeva's words, "[t]he foreigner is within us" (1991: 191). Invested with a mixture of vulnerability and honesty[19] he recognizes that his own foreignness is twofold: on the one hand, he is himself but the descendent of "recent" and "traceable" immigrants, and on the other, he is just a visitor "attuned, from far back, to 'European' importances" (James *AS* 1994: 103).

James's use of *Baedeker* during his American tour is a poignant indication of his estrangement. Likewise, when he asks for direction "of a flagrant foreigner," he further accentuates his own foreignness through the act of permuting his nativeness with the Armenian who is too confident to accept James's fraternal overtures (James *AS* 1994: 91–2). In New York, he is vanquished by alienation and feels a "flat fatigue" (James *AS* 1994: 93). Despite the hostility of some of the "aliens" who feel at home and who can dispense with a native's assistance, James still demonstrates a "fraternizing sense" (James *AS* 1994: 97). He also finds "comfort" in reckoning with the "defiant scale of numerosity and quantity," a process which allows him "to open . . . contingent doors and windows" (James *AS* 1994: 93). In the concluding pages of *The American Scene*, James presses the point that "[n]o kind of person . . . is a very good kind, . . . when its education has not been made to some extent by contact with other kinds, by a sense of the existence of other kinds, and, to that degree, by a certain relation with them" (James *AS* 1994: 315).

On two instances, James impersonates the Native American with a remarkable sense of empathy. While taking a walk in the precincts of the Capitol, he encounters "a trio of Indian braves . . . dispossessed of forest and prairie" (James *AS* 1994: 267), who remind him of the "brazen face of history" (James *AS* 1994: 268). In the very last passages of the book, he addresses America, chiding her for the "ravage" it has caused to the natives: "If I were one of the painted savages you have dispossessed . . . I should owe you my grudge for every disfigurement and every violence, for every wound with which you have caused the face of the land to bleed" (James *AS* 1994: 341).

In his preface to *A Little Tour in France*, James expresses his "regret that I might not have gone farther, penetrated deeper, spoken oftener – closed, in short, more intimately with the great general subject; and I mean, of course, not in a form as the present, but in many another, possible and impossible" (James *LT* 1900: v). *The American Scene*, is the opportunity James seized to expiate his remorse and to consummate what he had failed to accomplish in his record of French travel. Autoethnography is probably one of the "possible and impossible" "forms" James aspired to achieve.

Notes

1 *A Little Tour in France* was based on James's 1882 six-week tour of French Provence. It was serialized in *The Atlantic Monthly* between 1883 and 1884. It first appeared in book form in 1884, and a second revised edition followed in 1900.
2 Most of the material in *Italian Hours* appeared as essays in the early 1870s.
3 This is Joan-Pau Rubiés's phrase. See his (2002) "Travel Writing and Ethnography," *The Cambridge Companion to Travel Writing*, edited by Peter Hulme and Tim Young, Cambridge and New York: Cambridge University Press: 242.
4 Chronotopicity is Bakhtin's word. See (1981) *The Dialogic Imagination*, Austin: University of Texas Press: 97.
5 For a detailed study of the number of labels applied to travel writing, see Jan Born, "Defining Travel: On the Travel Book, Travel Writing and Terminology," *Perspectives on Travel Writing*, edited by Glenn Hooper and Tim Youngs, Aldershot: Ashgate: 13–26.
6 For Bal, Chaillou, Chupeau, Todorov, de Certeau, and others, movement in space and exploration of sites yields clues as to how narratives operate. See Mieke Bal (1997), *Narratology: Introduction to the Theory of Narrative*, Toronto: University of Toronto Press; Michel Chaillou (1992), "La mer, la route, la poussière," *Pour une littérature voyageuse*, edited by Alain Borer, Nicolas Bouvier, et al., Bruxelles: Éditions Complexe: 57–81; Jacques Chupeau (1977), "Les récits de voyages aux lisières du roman," *Revue d'Histoire littéraire de la France*, vol. 3, no. 4: 536–53; and Michel de Certeau (1984), *The Practice of Everyday Life*, translated by Steven Rendall, Berkeley: University of California Press.
7 This is David Herman's phrase. See his (1997) "Scripts, Sequences, and Stories: Elements of Postclassical Narratology," *PMLA*, vol. 112, no. 5, October: 1046.
8 Even *Italian Hours*, which purports to be a travel book, vacillates between the guide and the travel book proper. James uses phrases which echo a *Baedeker* or a *Murray* such as "I recommend you to look out for of a fine afternoon" (James *IH* 1909: 148), or tries to convince the reader "that Albano is worth a walk" (James *IH* 1909: 179).
9 When James reached the Midi, he wrote to his brother William "I pursued my pilgrimage through these rather dull French towns and through a good deal of bad weather, and all my desire now is to bring it to a prompt conclusion. It is rather dreary work" (qtd. in Edel 1985: 282).

10 Most Probably *Les Environs de Paris* (1868) by Adolphe Joanne.
11 James used photographs to stimulate his memory. He confessed: "So I have not the memory of Chinon; I have only the regret. But regret, as well as memory, has its visions; especially when, like memory, it is assisted by photographs" (James *LT* 1900: 68).
12 James might have been influenced by his brother William James's work on emotion, which was mostly characterized by an emphasis on experience and which was tightly linked to the stream of consciousness technique.
13 See especially the preface to the Second Edition (1997) of Harold Bloom's *The Anxiety of Influence: A Theory of Poetry*, New York: Oxford University Press.
14 Also see Bloom's preface.
15 See J. W. Cross, ed (1968) *George Eliot's Life as Related in Her Letters and Journals*. 3 vols, London: Blackwood, 1885, Boston: Dana Estes.
16 See for instance Rubiès's "Travel Writing and Ethnography," *The Cambridge Companion to Travel Writing*, edited by Peter Hulme and Tim Young, Cambridge and New York: Cambridge University Press: 242–60.
17 Carolyn Ellis (2004) argues that autoethnography involves "concrete action, dialogue, emotion, embodiment, spirituality and self-consciousness." See her *The Ethnographic I: A Methodological Novel about Autoethnography*, Walnut Creek, CA: AltaMira Press: 38.
18 Brian Richardson (2006) identifies the "interlocutor" as a surrogate of an "extreme narrating mode." See his *Unnatural Voices: Extreme Narration in Modern and Contemporary Fiction*, Ohio: Ohio State University Press: 79.
19 These are Bochner's terms. See his (2016) *Evocative Autoethnography: Writing Lives and Telling Stories*, New York: Routledge: 213.

Bibliography

Bakhtin, Mikhail (1981) "Forms of Time and of the Chronotope in the Novel," *The Dialogic Imagination: Four Essays*, edited by Michael Holoquist, translated by Caryl Emerson and Michael Holoquist, Austin: University of Texas Press: 84–258.

Behar, Ruth (1996) *The Vulnerable Observer: Anthropology that Breaks your Heart*, Boston: Beacon Press.

Bellanca, Mary Ellen (1997) "Recollecting Nature: George Eliot's 'Ilfracombe Journal' and Victorian Women's Natural History Writing," *Modern Language Studies*, vol. 27, no. 3–4, Autumn–Winter: 19–36.

Bentley, Nancy (1995) *The Ethnography of Manners: Hawthorne, James, Wharton*, Cambridge, New York and Melbourne: Cambridge University Press.

Bloom, Harold (1997) *The Anxiety of Influence: A Theory of Poetry*, New York: Oxford University Press.

Bochner, Arthur (2016) *Evocative Autoethnography: Writing Lives and Telling Stories*, New York: Routledge.

Born, Jan (2004) "Defining Travel: On the Travel Book, Travel Writing and Terminology," *Perspectives on Travel Writing*, edited by Glenn Hooper and Tim Youngs, Aldershot: Ashgate Publishing Co: 13–26.

Buelens, Gert (1999) "James's 'Aliens': Consuming, Performing, and Judging *The American Scene*," *Modern Philology*, vol. 96, no. 3. February: 347–63.

Butor, Michel (2001) "Travel and Writing," *Defining Travel: Diverse Visions*, edited by Susan L. Roberson, translated by John Powers and K. Lisker, Jackson: University Press of Mississippi: 69–87.

Buzard, James (2002) "The Grand Tour and After (1660–1840)," *The Cambridge Companion to Travel Writing*, edited by Hulme, Peter and Tim Young, Cambridge and New York: Cambridge University Press: 37–52.

Caesar, Terry (1995) *Forgiving the Boundaries: Home as Abroad in American Travel Writing*, Athens, GA: University of Georgia Press.

Duncan, James and Derek Gregory (1999) "Introduction," *Writes of Passage: Reading Travel Writing*, edited by James S. Duncan and Derek Gregory, London and New York: Routledge: 1–13.

Edel, Leon (1985) *Henry James: A Life*. New York: Harper & Row.

Eliot, George (1998a) "Recollections of Italy," *The Journals of George Eliot*, edited by Margaret Harris and Judith Johnston, Cambridge: Cambridge University Press: 327–68. Originally published 1885.

——— (1998b) "Recollections of Ilfracombe," *The Journals of George Eliot*, edited by Margaret Harris and Judith Johnston, Cambridge: Cambridge University Press: 259–73. Originally published 1885.

Ellis, Carolyn (2004) *The Ethnographic I: A Methodological Novel about Autoethnography,* Walnut Creek, CA: AltaMira Press.

Ellis, Carolyn, Tony E. Adams and Arthur P. Bochner (2011) "Autoethnography: An Overview," *Forum: Qualitative Social Research*, no. 12, January: 1–18.

Herman, David (1997) "Scripts, Sequences, and Stories: Elements of Postclassical Narratology," *PMLA*, vol. 112, no. 5, October: 1046–59.

Holland, Patrick and Graham Huggan (2000) *Tourists with Typewriters: Critical Reflections on Contemporary Travel Writing*, Ann Arbor, MI: University of Michigan Press.

Holman-Jones Stacy (2000) "Autoethnography: Making the Personal Political," *Handbook of Qualitative Research*, edited by N. K. Denzin and Y. S. Lincoln, Thousand Oaks, CA: Sage: 763–90.

Hooper, Glenn and Tim Youngs, eds. (2004) "Introduction," *Perspectives on Travel Writing*, Aldershot and Vermont: Ashgate Publishing Co: 1–12.

Hulme, Peter and Tim Young, eds. (2002) *The Cambridge Companion to Travel Writing*, Cambridge and New York: Cambridge University Press.

James, Henry (1909) *Italian Hours*, London: Heinemann.

——— (1920) *The Letters of Henry James*, edited by Percy Lubbock, New York: Charles Scribner's Sons.

——— (1961) *The Notebooks of Henry James*, edited by F. O. Matthiessen and Kenneth B. Murdock, New York: Oxford University Press.

——— (1970) "The Life of George Eliot," *Partial Portraits by Henry James*, edited by Leon Edel, Ann Arbor, MI: University of Michigan Press: 37–62. Reprinted from the Atlantic Monthly, 55 (May 1885): 668–78.

——— (1974) *Letters 1843–1875*, vol. 1, Cambridge, MA: Harvard University Press.

——— (1909) *A Little Tour in France*, Boston and New York: Houghton Mifflin and Company.

———— (1994) *The American Scene*, edited by John F. Sears, New York: Penguin Books. Originally published 1907.

Joanne, Adolphe (1868) *Les Environs de Paris, Paris*: Hachette et Cie.

Kristeva, Julia (1991) *Strangers to Ourselves*, translated by Leon S. Roudiez, New York: Columbia University Press.

Posnock, Ross (1991) *The Trial of Curiosity: Henry James, William James, and the Challenge of Modernity*, Oxford and New York: Oxford University Press.

Reed-Danahay, D. E. (1997) "Introduction." *Auto/Ethnography: Rewriting the Self and the Social*, edited by D. E. Reed-Danahay. Oxford: Berg: 1–17.

Richardson, Brian (2006) *Unnatural Voices: Extreme Narration in Modern and Contemporary Fiction*, Columbus, OH: Ohio State University Press.

Rubiés, Joan Pau (2002) "Travel Writing and Ethnography," *The Cambridge Companion to Travel Writing*, edited by Peter Hulme and Tim Young, Cambridge and New York: Cambridge University Press: 242–60.

Schriber, Mary Suzanne (1997) *Writing Home: American Women Abroad, 1830–1920*, Charlottesville and London: University Press of Virginia.

Viviès, Jean (2002) *English Narratives in the Eighteenth Century: Exploring Genres*, translated by Claire Davison, Aldershot and Burlington, VT: Ashgate Publishing Co.

4   Roderick's body, Winckelmann, and the screen of the touristic gaze

Geoff Bender

Within the first chapter of *Roderick Hudson*, Henry James gives us one of the most seductive passages in his entire oeuvre – the description of a nude young man fashioned as a statue. "The attitude was perfectly simple," James writes.

> The lad was squarely planted on his feet, with his legs a little apart; his back was slightly hollowed, his head thrown back, and both hands raised to support [a] rustic cup. There was a loosened fillet of wild flowers about his head, and his eyes, under their drooped lids, looked straight into the cup. On the base was scratched the Greek word Δίψα, Thirst.
>
> (1986: 59)

Given the paucity of models in provincial Northampton, Massachusetts, where the sculptor, Roderick Hudson, first plied his craft, the model for *Thirst* was likely none other than Roderick himself. In neighbor Cecilia's well-appointed little parlor, then, Roderick stood in bronze, offering himself to two kinds of contemplation simultaneously. Publically, he posed as an aesthetic object to be admired for his form and symmetry. Privately, he presented himself as a mute but potent erotic object to be delectated by viewers such as Rowland Mallet, who looked at him and fell in love, to their mutual destruction. Crucially, the tension James gives us in *Thirst* between aesthetic and erotic attractions relies on an emphatically classical body ideal, which, to nineteenth-century audiences, alone could present nudity to a refined sensibility as an object of uplift, thus permitting the long look with its covert possibility of erotic absorption.

Further, by situating Roderick's body in a book spanning two continents and seemingly endless conversations on the antique, James vigorously engaged the Anglo-American travel book, whose praise of the classical aesthetic was repeatedly intoned by self-proclaimed connoisseurs seeking to educate the middle-class masses in the proper taste. Nineteenth-century travel writers revered, and taught their readers to revere, classicism as the foundation of aesthetic virtue in a visual world where purity of design – what Bayard Taylor called, in his *Views Afoot* (1846), a "glorious perfection of form" – was the hallmark of the virtuous sculptural body (1854: 324). Most virtuous in the classical pantheon travel writers dwelt on was the Apollonian young man, cut in marble or cast in bronze, unencumbered by a compulsory modesty and unabashed in a naiveté that was as close as the Victorian imagination could come to the unfallen state. And so Roderick stood, erotically charged and aesthetically ideal, his nudity made benign by a correctly adjusted connoisseurial eye – until, at the novel's end, the aesthetic frame snapped by an act of self-consciousness that decomposed both Roderick's beauty and the erotic regard his beauty enabled.

Sexual purity, classicism, and the touristic gaze

The masculine eroticism that a popularized classical aesthetic made available to the American bourgeois imagination, and that James so intriguingly played with in his first significant novel, emerged out of fraught circumstances in nineteenth-century debates over what constituted bodily and thus moral purity. A brief history of this debate and of the ways in which the winning side encoded erotic reactions in aesthetic response is crucial to a deep reading of the erotic role of classicism in *Roderick Hudson*. On one side of the divide were American artists like Erastus Dowe Palmer, who argued that classical statuary revealed "the purest and best of our nature" (1856: 18), and so figured purity in idealized human nudity. On the other side were health reformers such as Sylvester Graham, who took the opposite point of view. The body, for Graham, was inimical to middle-class probity for its relentless and "depraved" craving after satisfaction of the physical "appetites," particularly the sexual appetite, which led, most problematically, to "self-pollution" – a debility men were thought particularly vulnerable to (1837: 56, 59, 139). Indulged bodies conduced, Graham argued, "to the worst of consequences" (1837: 59), among them

> feebleness of circulation, chilliness, head-ache, melancholy, hypochondria, hysterics, feebleness of all the senses, impaired vision, loss of sight, weakness of the lungs, nervous cough, pulmonary consumption, disorders of the liver and kidneys, urinary difficulties, disorders of the genital organs, spinal diseases, weakness of the brain, loss of memory, epilepsy, insanity, [and] apoplexy.

(1837: 69)

For Graham and his purist cohort, an unpolluted body was barely a body at all, kept alive by "a plain, simple, unstimulating, vegetable and water diet" of "not excessive quantity" (1837: 139–140). And so while Palmer insisted that the classical nude revealed a human's "pure, elevated, and Godlike" state (1856: 19), nineteenth-century sexual purists saw in such examples of high art only "infernal efforts" made to degrade the "thoughts and affections" of youth, so that they were left permanently "impure" through a distinctly visual form of overstimulated appetite (Alcott 1849: 331).

The most famous nineteenth-century American flashpoint in this debate was likely Hiram Powers's neoclassical *Greek Slave* (1843) (Figure 4.1), which depicted a white woman stripped to be sold at a Turkish auction

Figure 4.1 The Greek Slave by Hiram Powers (1844/1850). © Yale University Art Gallery.

though she was, Powers insisted in an explanatory pamphlet, "too deeply concerned" over her fate "to be aware of her nakedness" (qtd. in Crane 1972: 204). Purist reviews of the *Greek Slave* on exhibition didn't, however, agree. Echoing Graham and his ilk, a review for Ohio's *Western Christian Advocate* (29 Nov. 1848) was typical. Replying with a clear Evangelical note of warning to all who would see it, the author decried: "[T]he exhibition of the Greek Slave, in our humble judgment, prepares the way for the model artist; and they for the house which leads to the chambers of death, and to the gates of hell" (qtd. in Wunder 1991: 233). For this nineteenth-century bourgeois author, the whorehouse, and eternal damnation thereafter, were but a few steps away from a willingness to gaze at a naked woman cut in marble.

However, reviews more persuasive to the cultured milieu legitimized the classical nude as a work of art, and the *Greek Slave* as a particularly fine example of such work, finding in a combination of affect and aesthetics a guarantor of visual upliftment, thereby abrogating an overtly erotic response to sculptural nudity that caused Evangelic social guardians such dismay. The Unitarian minister Orville Dewey offered a reaction that became exemplary of the kind of refinement the middle class aspired to. Denying the statue's nakedness entirely, Dewey exclaims melodramatically: "The *Greek Slave* is clothed all over with sentiment; sheltered, protected by it from every profane eye. Brocade, cloth of gold, could not be a more complete protection than the vesture of holiness in which she stands" (1847: 160). For middle-class audiences, Dewey's sentimentalism intertwined effectively with Palmer's idealism to fashion the neoclassical statue as an agent of moral purification rather than degradation. Looking at her, then, became the antithesis of a self-damning act.

Significantly, Dewey was the author of an important nineteenth-century American travel book, *The Old World and the New* (1836), whose conventions prepared him to see the *Greek Slave* as exalted. The sensibility he cultivated in that book is what John Urry has called the product of the "tourist gaze": a way of seeing that provides a "cognitive and perceptual education" for both the exemplary tourist-author and those readers who wish they could be (1990: 4). Dewey's touristic gaze, tuned by his travels, enabled his sentimentalist covering of the statue's nakedness. To underscore this point, compare his description of the *Greek Slave*, above, with his praise of the *Venus de Medici*, an antique prototype that he viewed at the Uffizi in Florence. "The Venus," he muses, "is held to be the model of beauty, and beautiful enough it is, and the beauty grows upon one at every repeated view" (Dewey 1836: 54). In this passage Dewey first presents conventional aesthetic wisdom – that the Venus is "held to be" beautiful by those who know – then models an internalization of that wisdom: the statue "grows" in "beauty" at every fresh encounter or "repeated view." By such a process, Dewey demonstrates an acquired cultural sophistication and, further, illustrates for his readers the process by which they can do the same, provided that they gaze at the right work in the right way. The beauty Dewey comes to see as intrinsic to the naked Venus then becomes materialized as an aesthetic "vesture of holiness" that, he persuades his readers, clothes the *Greek Slave*'s otherwise divested form. His pronouncements were, of course, riddled with touristic clichés, but they were clichés his readers took seriously so as to reflect a travelled sensibility required by an upwardly mobile middle class seeking to leave their provincial roots in acts of social ascension.

Of course, the attraction of the classical aesthetic clearly exceeded an interest in the proper style. Through it, an otherwise sexually repressed and prudish class could attend to sexual yearning without moral censure, while appearing to be engaged in acts of aesthetic purification. Viewing classical statuary thus fed the erotic imagination, producing reactions ranging from mild titillation, as in Dewey's religiosity, to something more physically entailed. In an 1847 article in *Neal's Saturday Gazette*, for example, Clara Cushman recorded a response to the *Greek Slave* that outdid Dewey's modest blush. "[A]h, it is a woman," she exclaims,

> and Pygmalion-like, the artist has given to her a soul. For the first time I could enter into the spirit of that beautiful fable. I could imagine the devotion with which the statue was gazed upon, day by day, as its development progressed beneath his skilful [*sic*] hand – the delicate stroke chiming faintly to his fast coming fancies, as the chisel rang upon that pure surface – how he had dwelt upon its perfections until he grew mad with love for the creation of his own genius!
>
> (1848: 29)

While Cushman imagines Powers as Pygmalion, it seems plain that Cushman, too, has grown "mad with love" for the statue. As she gazes on its surfaces, "flushing" with a "rosy tinge," it is her own sexual "flushing" that seems to grow from a "train of dreamy, delicious revery [*sic*]" until she "could have wept with a perfect agony of tears" (1848: 29). Cushman's agony is also her ecstasy, clearly; her prose builds to an orgasmic intensity. However, the sexual dimension of Cushman's experience remains camouflaged behind an apparent engagement with the statue's aesthetic content. Her sexual ecstasy therefore could not likely have been seen as such by her contemporaries. It "fall[s] aslant of" the period's "codes," as Peter Coviello says, by which sex is "discursively constituted" (2013: 11). Her experience is not just erotic, breaking the code of women's passionlessness

(Cott 1978: 221), but homoerotic, engendering a double taboo. And so her overwhelmment could only have been accounted for by an aesthetic, not an erotic, suffusion.

After her climactic moment, Cushman returns us readers to earth in markedly more measured tones. She concludes: "[T]he simplicity and purity with which the form is veiled as it were, takes from the mind every emotion save that of admiration" (1848: 29). Today even a casual gloss of Cushman's remarks is enough to suggest that she's done much more than just "admire" the woman in front of her. Her comment rings hollow more now than then, especially when seen through the lens of what Jack Halberstam famously calls our own "perverse presentism," in which we "apply insights from the present to conundrums of the past" to illuminate aspects of the past we can better see (1998: 53–4). One such insight is the presence of a fluidity of temper that allows Cushman to move from the erotic to the disinterested so mercurially, an attitude that, as David Greven has argued, pervades nineteenth-century literary work and "is a resonant indication of the instability of gender ideologies" during that period, before their "hardening into hard and fast national archetypes of the American 'man' and 'woman'" after the turn of the twentieth century (2014: 12). Here, then, is an example of such instability, as Cushman first explodes with a yearning for the woman before her that, a few beats later, recedes into sentiments of conventional propriety. For mid-nineteenth-century readers, this metamorphosis would likely have read as yet another instantiation of the sentimentally imbued tearful moment, entirely expected of a moving experience of art.

Thus Venus, either as the classical *Venus de Medici* or the neoclassical *Greek Slave*, provided a means by which members of middle-class culture could experience their desires for female bodies in a way that largely masked their anxieties about these bodies and their concomitant sexual provocations. It was, however, the Apollo, Venus's nineteenth-century classical counterpart, that benefited from a kind of aesthetic depth that had no complement in Venusian discourse – a depth that preceded and was then coopted by the ascending American middle class. Indeed, if the nineteenth-century taste for Apollonian young men had to be given a point of origin, that point would probably be somewhere in the work of the eighteenth-century German art historian Johann Joachim Winckelmann.

Winckelmann and Apollo's queer beauty

Winckelmann is best known today for his aphoristic understanding of what makes the best in ancient Greek statuary: that it is possessed of "a noble simplicity and quiet grandeur" (Winckelmann 1987: 35), a passage found in his brief work *Reflections on the Imitation of Greek Works in Painting and Sculpture* (1755). In his farther-reaching *History of the Art of Antiquity* (1764), however, Winckelmann laid out more elaborate terms by which "simplicity" and "grandeur" could inform the most beautiful Hellenic bodies, which, for Winckelmann, were epitomized in the bodies of young men, specifically, the ancient sculptural renderings of Apollo. In Apollo, Winckelmann wrote, "is combined the vigor of maturity with the soft forms of the most beautiful springtime of youth. . . . Thus, Apollo was the most beautiful of the gods. Health flourishes in this youth, and vigor makes itself felt, like the dawn of a beautiful day" (2006: 200). It was a sentiment with deeply erotic underpinnings reflecting a set of aesthetic "priorities," which, as Francis Haskell and Nicholas Penny remind us, "prevailed throughout Europe and America" from the late eighteenth century on, largely due to the widely recognized gravitas of Winckelmann's judgement (1981: 107). Crucially, Winckelmann's homoerotic sentiment was imported and purveyed by nineteenth-century American travel book writers, who relied on Continental art historians like Winckelmann for their substance. Winckelmann was, in a sense, a connoisseur's connoisseur; his aesthetic assessments thus became assurances of expertise to writers who imitated him until they killed him, as Haskell and Penny underscore, in "cliché" (1981: 146).

Like the aesthetic discourse that shaped a bourgeois viewing of the *Greek Slave*, Winckelmannian philhellenism provided travel writers with the means to rhapsodize with the kind of erotic awe that readers like Cushman would later replicate, in an American context, so faithfully. Thus Orville Dewey himself, considerably more impressed by the Vatican's *Apollo Belvedere* (Figure 4.2) than by the Uffizi's *Medici Venus*, exalts:

> What the beauty and power of this unequalled statue is, it would be utterly impossible for me to express; it would be folly to attempt it. What a divinity of beauty, what a sovereignty of intellect, what dignity of conscious power, is stamped upon every feature! You can hardly persuade yourself, as you gaze upon it, that there is not an actual *glow* upon the cheek and brow. For my own part, I am paralyzed by this wonderful work, so often as I see it. I sit down and gaze upon it, in a sort of revery, and do not know but I sometimes say aloud, "Oh! Heaven!" – for really it is difficult to resist exclamations and tears.
>
> (1836: 107–8)

Like Cushman, Dewey's "revery" ends in "tears," but unlike Cushman, Dewey's "revery" is punctuated by an "Oh! Heaven!" that is nothing less than ejaculatory, in several senses of that word.

Figure 4.2 Apollo Belvedere by Leochares (c. 350–325 BCE). © Vanni Archive / Art Resource, NY.

Perhaps the most homoerotically charged touristic account of the Apollo was penned by Dewey's contemporary, Nathaniel Parker Willis. In his *Pencillings by the Way* (1836), Willis too beholds the *Apollo Belvedere* at the Vatican as "a god-like model of a man." Willis, though, is more markedly fixated on the androgynous contours of the Apollo's body, paying little evident notice to his "sovereignty of intellect." Enraptured, he declares:

The lightness and the elegance of the limbs; the free, fiery, confident energy of the attitude; the breathing, indignant nostril and lips; the whole statue's mingled and equal grace and power, are, with all its truth to nature, beyond any conception I had formed of manly beauty. It spoils one's eye for common men to look at it. It stands there like a descended angel, with a splendor of form and an air of power, that makes one feel what he should have been, and mortifies him for what he is.

(1853: 303)

In his astute reading of Winckelmannian discourse, *Flesh and the Ideal: Winckelmann and the Origins of Art History* (1994), Alex Potts explains the peculiarly Winckelmannian character of Willis's erotic overwhelmment. "In Winckelmann," Potts writes,

the spectator's identifying with the irresistibly dominating figure confronting him eventually reaches the point at which his sense of self is effectively annihilated. The spectator is taken over by the all-powerful other: or, to put it in Winckelmann's terms, the god enters and gains possession of the spectator and makes him its mouthpiece.

(1994: 127)

This is Willis's paradox precisely: he desires to see himself mirrored in a figure that at once resembles him and differs from him dramatically. Thus Willis's identification with the same-sex god gives over to near-annihilation by that god in an attitude of passive submission to the god's superior power, his *virtus*, as Apollo "enters" him to "possess" him absolutely and erotically.

Willis's and Dewey's erotic accounts of their encounters with the Apollo are clear instantiations of what Whitney Davis has called the "queer beauty" within mainstream bourgeois culture: the presence of "aesthetic ideals" – here, via the optically available naked man – that both "claim validity within an entire society" and are "based on manifestly homoerotic prototypes and significance" (2010: 23). What is remarkable about such queer moments in mainstream culture, for Davis, is the "normative communalization of judgments of taste" that works of art, like the *Apollo Belvedere*, inspire. The queer yet manly beauty of statuary like the *Apollo* and, later, the *Adorante* attained a "wide social assent" so as to reflect "an entire community's ideals *of* itself *for* itself" (Davis 2010: 27, emphasis original). We see, then, nineteenth-century, bourgeois American men's aspirational perfectionism expressed as a widespread social phenomenon that celebrated imagined versions of their own bodies as objects they could adore. And more than that, as bodies – as other men's bodies – that could arouse them in profoundly physical ways. Dewey's "revery" and Willis's "mortifi[cation]" are both synonyms for sexual climax, in the context of their encomiums to the *Apollo*; these expressions mark out a queer erotics that could be publically enjoyed, even prescribed to bourgeois readers – all while it remained hidden in plain sight.

Making Roderick's body: from Apollo to the *Adorante*

The Apollonian figure of Roderick Hudson, presented in self-portrait as *Thirst*, with his "squarely planted" feet, his "slightly hollowed" back, and his "droop[ing] lids," could not be said to be a direct transcription either of Winckelmann's Apollo or of the travel books that worshipped him. But Roderick, as the classical nude that structures James's novel, is no less Winckelmannian, no less the product of the touristic gaze, and no less queer for this lack. For though Winckelmann might have epitomized beautiful manhood in the Apollo, elsewhere in his *History* he broadens the range to include other beautiful male bodies within the realm of the Apollonian. This point is especially emphasized in a popular Victorian-era translation of Winckelmann's *History* by G. Henry Lodge, which states:

> The first, or male ideal, has its different degrees. It begins in the young Satyrs or Fauns, as humble conceptions of divinities. The most beautiful statues of Fauns present to us an image of ripe, beautiful youth, in perfect proportion. . . . [Indeed, they are] so shaped, that each one of them, if it were not for the head, might be mistaken for an Apollo.
>
> (Lodge 1872: 323)

What's noteworthy here is a division between what Davis, summarizing the work of classical scholars, calls the "high style," associated with the sculptor Phidias and characterized by a "supreme ideal beauty" tending toward "grandeur" and severity, and a softer version of an already androgynous masculinity associated with the sculptor Praxiteles and characterized by a more "ephebic" and "feminized" male body (2010: 34–5). Between Phidias and Praxiteles, then, is a continuum of erotically charged masculine bodies that conform to a flexible rendering of bodily shape. And yet, Winckelmann seems to insist that the difference between "high" and "ephebic" masculinities comes down to nothing more than a head. In other words, the bodies of "ripe, beautiful youth," broadly termed Apollonian, can be as muscular as they are faunlike, as heroic as they are soft and still suit the ideal.

For an exemplar of the latter form of Apollonian ideality, no statue was more convincing to late-nineteenth-century sensibilities than the classical bronze *Adorante*, otherwise known as the *Praying Boy* (Figure 4.3). Less vigorous than the *Belvedere Apollo*, the *Adorante* was yet deeply invested with the androgynous Apollonian ideal. An 1871 edition of *Murray's Handbook* simply called it "one of the finest antique bronze statues in existence" (1871: 352). This statue, owned in turn by Charles I, Louis XIV, and Frederick II before being seized by Napoleon, was on display, in James's time,

Figure 4.3 Adorante ("Praying Boy") by Lysippos (380–310 BCE). © bpk Bildagentur / Antikensammlung, Staaliche Museen / Jahannes Laurentius / Art Resource, NY.

in Berlin, where *Murray's* urged travellers to see it. Unlike *Murray's*, Walter Pater, in his *Studies in the History of the Renaissance* (1873), had far more than a sentence of praise for the figure. In a chapter on Winckelmann, he revelled in the statue's beauty for pages. To Pater, the *Adorante* coalesced "in a single instance" an "unclassified purity of life, with its blending and interpenetration of intellectual, spiritual, and physical elements, still folded together, pregnant with the possibilities of a whole world closed within it" (1873: 191). Thus, like Roderick's *Thirst*, the *Adorante* is, for Pater, supremely and beautifully naïve: "the image of man as he springs first from the sleep of nature; his white light taking no colour from any one-sided experience, characterless so far as character involves subjection to the accidental influences of life" (1873: 191–2). As a synthesis of "intellect" with the "physical elements," Pater's *Adorante* also echoes earlier, touristic encomiums to the *Apollo*: Dewey's "sovereignty of intellect," for example, and Willis's "lightness and . . . elegance of . . . limbs."

Scholars have persuasively suggested that James was reading, and deeply influenced by, Pater's *Renaissance* while writing *Roderick Hudson* (Ellman 1984: 210; Freedman 1990: 133). Pater's *Adorante* quite reasonably serves as a palimpsest not just for *Thirst* but for Roderick's live body as well. If Apollonian beauty is defined by a range of possible body forms, from the ephebic to the heroic, then Roderick's body certainly leans toward the ephebic end of the scale: he is beautiful without possessing a godlike potency or an "air of power," as Willis would say. When the narrator tells us that his voice streams from a "soft and not altogether masculine organ" (James *RH* 1986: 63), it's hard not to think of what other organ Roderick might possess that is also "soft and not altogether masculine." Yet his phallic indeterminacy lends him an ephebic sort of attractiveness. Still, there is "life enough in his eye to furnish an immortality," all while Roderick's "whole structure" is exceedingly "narrow": his "forehead," his "jaw," his "shoulders," as if composed of "insufficient physical substance" (James *RH* 1986: 64). Made of both "boyish unconsciousness and manly shrewdness" (James *RH* 1986: 65), Roderick's living, breathing presence is as androgynous as his statue. His precise resemblance to Pater's *Adorante* – "naïve" and "unperplexed" for want of "the accidental influences of life" (Pater 1873: 191–2) – certainly accounts for Roderick's youthful "unconsciousness." His "manly shrewdness," on the other hand, requires aesthetic material from a different part of the Apollonian continuum, some facial trace from the *Apollo Belvedere*'s "intensity of expression," as Dewey put it, which accounted in physiognomic terms for the Apollo's ostensible "sovereignty of intellect" (1836: 107).

Just as the ephebic plays a dominant role in the making of Roderick's body, so it also plays a major part in undoing it. The ephebe is a naïf, and naiveté links Roderick to the otherwise urbane Christina Light, Roderick's putative love object, who, like Roderick, thinks she knows more than she does. Their shared naiveté is established physiognomically, through common portrait features. In carving her bust, Roderick in many ways recreates his own. Tellingly, Light's portrait at once registers Winckelmann literally and also emblematizes the Winckelmannian aesthetic that has informed the visual structure of the text. Of Christina's bust, the narrator says: "The resemblance was deep and vivid; there was extreme fidelity of detail, and yet *a noble simplicity*. One could say of the head that, without idealization, it was a representation of ideal beauty" (James *RH* 1986: 165, my emphasis). Christina's bust is unambiguously Winckelmannian in its "noble simplicity," a key Winckelmannian tag, but it also registers Winckelmann at deeper levels, in the paradox of an image that is "ideal" but not "ideali[zed]" – a feat thought impossible in neoclassical sculpture. Conventionally, it was the sculptor's job to take a subject from nature and refashion it into ideal proportions, for no such perfection, it was thought, existed in unmitigated nature. As the neoclassical critic Joshua Reynolds wrote in his *Discourses on Art* (1797): "[A]ll the arts receive their perfection from an ideal beauty, superior to what is to be found in individual nature" (1997: 42). Idealization was the process by which the "arts" articulated this "perfection." The mystery of Christina's beauty – and also of Roderick's beauty – is that it is "perfection" that is not "superior to" or beyond nature. Therefore, her bust and Roderick's self-portrait in *Thirst* are quotations *from* nature; as such, they are representations of the impossible: perfect nature.

And yet, while Reynolds might object, to be "ideal" without "idealisation" is precisely what Davis has identified as Winckelmann's "anti-Platonic" Platonism (2010: 29), a working contradiction that Davis compellingly characterizes as "the continuous movements of desire toward ideality, in ideality, and around ideality" (2010: 30). While Plato holds ideal beauty to be beyond bodily representation, however much it might be hinted at by that representation – the mere "namesake" of the "absolute," as he says in the *Phaedrus* (1973: 57) – Winckelmann maintains that desire propels the sculptor "beyond the ideal" (Davis 2010: 30) in order to shape ideal form in concrete matter. For such shaping to make sense, Winckelmannian perfection needs to be a dynamic entity unencumbered by a static "absolute." A neoclassical sculptor such as Erastus Dowe Palmer idealized a body in marble to immortalize it and, consequently, left an immutable shape – static, by necessity. Stone, after all, doesn't move. As a concrete representation, it could not be the Platonic absolute, but it could gesture at the absolute through the presentation of a form that could not exist in nature. An ancient sculptor, on the other hand, such as Praxiteles or Phidias, possessed a different sort of power, following this Winckelmannian line. He could cut the ideal in marble in a way that rendered it both dynamic and mutable to the optical engagement of a viewer's desire. The marble of such statuary was thus never quite solid and never gestured toward a static, incorporeal absolute. Instead, it moved. It informed a corporeal design ever altering before a desiring eye. "It is these movements" of desire, Davis concludes, that, for Winckelmann, "constitute the primal conditions of knowing in a human being" (2010: 30). Obviously, such "primal conditions" present a deeper Winckelmann than touristic renderings of his aesthetics typically conveyed.

These subtle levels of Winckelmann's aesthetic understanding were arguably not lost on James, whose engagement with Pater assured this. In *The Renaissance*, Pater, too, found an identity between Winckelmann and an anti-Platonic Plato, producing a version of Winckelmann that, in Pater's words, existed outside of Christian ontological models, contained, instead, within a "wholly Greek" cosmology. Winckelmann's Plato is "represented," Pater asserts, by "that group of brilliant youths" who are "still uninfected by any spiritual sickness, finding the end of all endeavour in the aspects of the human form, the continual stir and motion of a comely human life." "[H]uman life," then, is characterized by and dependent on "motion," as must be its finest "represent[ations]" (Pater 1873: 151). It is an aesthetic sentiment so acutely Jamesian, James could not but have agreed, and said as much in, for example, his introduction to *The New York Edition* of *Portrait of a Lady* (1908), where he writes of the " 'moral' sense of a work of art" as being dependent "on the amount of felt life" the artist possesses while "producing it" (*NYE PL* 1908: ix–x). The virtue of a literary work, like the virtue of a statue, is thus dependent on a "vision" so suffused with "life" (*NYE PL* 1908: x) that the work *must* move – simply because it is alive. And so Roderick's body, in this anti-Platonic Platonic sense, in this Winckelmannian-Pateresque way, in both flesh and bronze, metamorphoses before the desiring gaze of those who behold him.

This is even the case, perhaps most especially the case, in the least likely of circumstances: when Roderick is no longer alive, after he has "fallen from a great height" at the book's end. "[W]hat Rowland saw," the narrator tells us, "on first looking at him was only a strangely serene expression of life. The eyes were those of a dead man, but in a short time, when Rowland had closed them, the whole face seemed to awake" (James *RH* 1986: 386). Though Roderick is lying statue-still, it is this Winckelmannian quality of life that makes the inert "awake," which earlier animated *Thirst*, and which yet refuses to abandon Roderick's body in its last statuesque moment. Somehow, Roderick's body remains ideal – at least, the parts Rowland can see – without idealization, possessed of a quality that surpasses formal perfection in the name of human desire or, more specifically, Rowland's erotic desire. In this final death tableau, James illustrates yet again how classical aesthetics and its twin, eroticism, can simultaneously make and unmake Roderick's body with beguiling intricacy.

Connoisseurship and the unmaking of Roderick

But though Roderick retains a portion of his classical ideality even in death, the features that enabled him to pose in Apollonian beauty are certainly gone. Still, even with Roderick's body in this markedly transitional state,

Rowland still wants him. With the painter, Sam Singleton, away to get help, Rowland stays with Roderick, looking: "The most rational of men" has become "for an hour the most passionate" (James *RH* 1986: 387). In the wilderness, before Roderick's shattered body, Rowland exposes himself. Or, rather, James exposes Rowland by tearing away the veneer of his connoisseurship. Among other consequences of this dramatic scene, we can see just how thin that veneer really is. Until the book's end, Roderick's body is strangely resistant to the cheapening effects of the connoisseurial gaze; now, no longer. James, however, has been glibly satirizing Rowland's connoisseurial stance throughout, casting his derivative attempts at Winckelmannian aesthetics as vocalizations of the conventional nineteenth-century travel writer.

But James's satirizing of Rowland's efforts at connoisseurship should not be taken to mean that James has lost sympathy with Rowland himself. And so connoisseurship, like so many other qualities in this dense, layered novel, is composed of a set of shifting valences. When Rowland's cousin, Cecilia, introduces Rowland to Roderick as "connoisseur" (James *RH* 1986: 63), her sense of connoisseurship is as Nancy Glazener defines it: a master of "secular tastemaking apparatus" that is "designed to produce . . . properly controlled bourgeois American citizens" (1997: 91–2). Cecilia thus emphasizes Rowland's ability to bestow cultural capital on works of art he deems worthy to provincials who know no better. Rowland's authority as a "secular tastemak[er]" is conveyed along the same current of touristic sensibility that Dewey and Willis demonstrated above. All three men have seen the great works abroad, and so are, by default, authorities at home. Because of his prior reading and travel, Rowland carries himself as one who knows and who is qualified to prescribe the ways in which less experienced "bourgeois American citizens" should see. Thus, while it's possible to view Rowland's dilettantism a "failed *flâneur[ie]*," as Michèle Mendelssohn has argued (2003: 513), or as "a *refinement* of rank consumerism," as Wendy Graham has suggested (1999: 107), in provincial Northampton, Massachusetts, Rowland's pronouncements are words to take seriously. When he deems Roderick's *Thirst* "very good indeed" (James *RH* 1986: 66), Roderick has, in effect, just received his first positive critical review.

And as the analyses of touristic accounts of classical bodies reveal above, "good," here, is polyvalent praise, nuanced in spite of Rowland's otherwise derivative cultural authority. Roderick's body is both well executed artistically and also satisfyingly "good" erotically, though that cannot be said as such. Rowland's connoisseurship thus masks and conveys desire in the same fashion as that expressed by Willis and Dewey. He becomes, in fact, a means by which James can comment on this form of nineteenth-century mainstream celebration of "queer beauty" by giving us a plain view of its hidden-in-plain-sight quality. One of the queerest aspects of the classicism Rowland so admires is found in the presence of a small detail: a "rustic cup" that the statue holds up luxuriantly. The cup makes *Thirst* a cupbearer, like Ganymede, the mythic boy lover of Zeus. The *Adorante*, too, was identified by nineteenth-century connoisseurs as a cupbearer (Davis 2010: 26). Though he holds no cup, the gesture of his upward moving hands was evidently enough to suggest one. The *Adorante* is thus queer, as *Thirst* is queer and, consequently, Roderick, *Thirst*'s model, is queer – at least until he "falls into heterosexuality" at the novel's end, as Leland Person has persuasively suggested (2002: 121). This point is worth dwelling on one beat more. Rowland's connoisseurship doesn't just provide him with a mask behind which to desire Roderick; it also provides Roderick, the desired object, with similar cover. Connoisseurship, in this sense, is not simply a unidirectional model that allows for homoerotic adoration to be expressed by a culturally sanctioned personage like Rowland. Instead, in this case, it enables reciprocal agency: for Roderick to erotically admire Rowland back.

Rowland's queer desire for Roderick has already been duly noted by scholars such as Robert K. Martin (1978: 101), Kelly Cannon (1994: 93), and Mendelssohn (2003: 514). What critics have been slower to point out is Roderick's erotic response to Rowland. Hugh Stevens comes closest when he comments that "gestures" between the two men, "which could be read as flirtational[,] elicit no violent reaction from either man, nor any particular narrative comment" (1998: 74). We could amplify this observation to suggest that the flirtational rapport between Roderick and Rowland is not just not rebuffed but quietly encouraged, one by the other. This encouragement is illustrated in casual scenes, like the one after the unveiling of Roderick's first important sculpture in Rome, his *Adam*, when the narrator tells us Roderick and Rowland "laugh for a month" at the "certain formulas of the connoisseurs" who come to appraise it (James *RH* 1986: 115). Rowland can't see, though we can, that the joke is partially on him, just as it's on Roderick, who seems equally as blind to the irony. But no matter. As long as the aesthetic frame, be it connoisseurial or Paterian, remains in place, the homoerotic rapport between these men can continue.

It's thus not the reduction of Roderick's body to Rowland's pat assessment that destroys him, but rather, in the end, Roderick's own self-consciousness. The dawning of this new self-awareness occurs during the last interchange between Roderick and Rowland, when Roderick suddenly recognizes that his treatment of Mary Garland "must have appeared simply hideous" to Rowland (James *RH* 1986: 378). Crucially, it's not Roderick's treatment of Mary, but rather his concern over how Rowland *perceives* that treatment that produces, within Roderick, an "aesthetic disgust at the graceless contour of his conduct" (James *RH* 1986: 379). Pushing what James might mean by "graceless contour," we see Roderick losing not just his characterological shape but also his classical physical proportions. This tiered loss is registered in a silence between the two men, when Roderick, hurrying off, "stopped and looked" at Rowland, "then" – after their long, speechless interchange – "abruptly turned and disappeared below the crest of a hill" (James *RH* 1986: 379). This is the last moment Rowland would see Roderick physically alive. Without the possibility of the perception of Roderick via a pristine classicism, the homoerotic contact between the two men, by whatever means that contact occurred, cannot be maintained – not, at least, until Roderick's death, when Roderick's body can be materially re-aestheticized so as to become the object of Rowland's final, passionate vigil.

In closing, it's worth noting just how aesthetics, as a cover for Rowland and Roderick's homoerotic affection, usefully helps to complete Hugh Stevens's solution to the problem of why "homoerotic expression" in *Roderick Hudson* was both "legible" and "enjoyed" by readers just as homosexuality was becoming pathologized as an identity. Stevens claims that the novel's homoerotic freedom is possible because, at the moment of the novel's publication, homosexuality was not yet "legible" as such – that that legibility would grow over subsequent decades (1998: 67–8). It's a claim that scholars like historian Thomas A. Foster dispute, however, arguing "that the *acts-versus-identities* pronouncement is an oversimplification made from the vantage point of modernity and focusing on psychological models at the expense of others" (2007: 8, emphasis original). In other words, even though readers of *Roderick Hudson* might not have been looking for homosexual identities, homosexuality of some kind would still likely have been "legible," and therefore shocking if it weren't mitigated by some other screen. That screen, as I have been arguing, is the classical aesthetic, which, as David Greven, among others, has maintained, "coded" homoerotic desire that would be recognizable as such to members of queer subcultures while remaining "within acceptable social parameters of taste and decorum" for mainstream bourgeois culture at large (2012: 189). Roderick's Apollonian body could thus be open to Rowland's long, admiring look, and no one passing by either man would think much of it.

Bibliography

Alcott, William A. (1849) *The Young Man's Guide*, Boston: T. R. Marvin. Originally published 1834.

Cannon, Kelly (1994) *Henry James and Masculinity: The Man at the Margins*, New York: St. Martin's Press.

Cott, Nancy F. (1978) "Passionlessness: An Interpretation of Victorian Sexual Ideology, 1790–1850," *Signs*, vol. 4, no. 2: 219–36.

Coviello, Peter (2013) *Tomorrow's Parties: Sex and the Untimely in Nineteenth-Century America*, New York: New York University Press.

Crane, Sylvia E. (1972) *White Silence: Greenough, Powers, and Crawford, American Sculptors in Nineteenth-Century Italy*, Coral Gables, FL: University of Miami Press.

Cushman, Clara (1848) [Essay on *Greek Slave*] *Powers' Statue of the Greek Slave.* Boston: Eastburn's Press: 29. Originally published in *Neal's Saturday Gazette*, 1847.

Davis, Whitney (2010) *Queer Beauty: Sexuality and Aesthetics from Winckelmann to Freud and Beyond*, New York: Columbia University Press.

Dewey, Orville (1836) *The Old World and the New; or, a Journal of Reflections and Observations Made on a Tour in Europe*, vol. 2, New York: Harper & Brothers.

—— (1847) "Powers' Statues," *The Union Magazine of Literature and Art*, vol. 1, no. 4: 160–1.

Ellman, Richard (1984) "Henry James Among the Aesthetes," *Proceedings of the British Academy*, vol. 69: 209–28.

Foster, Thomas A. (2007) "Introduction," *Long Before Stonewall: Histories of Same-Sex Sexuality in Early America*, edited by Thomas A. Foster, New York: New York University Press: 1–16.

Freedman, Jonathan (1990) *Professions of Taste: Henry James, British Aestheticism, and Commodity Culture*, Stanford: Stanford University Press.

Glazener, Nancy (1997) *Reading for Realism: The History of a U.S. Literary Institution, 1850–1910*, Durham and London: Duke University Press.

Graham, Sylvester (1837) *A Lecture to Young Men, on Chastity: Intended also for the Serious Consideration of Parents and Guardians*, Boston: Light & Stearns. Originally published 1834.

Graham, Wendy (1999) *Henry James's Thwarted Love*, Stanford: Stanford University Press.

Greven, David (2012) *The Fragility of Manhood: Hawthorne, Freud, and the Politics of Gender*, Columbus, OH: Ohio State University Press.

—— (2014) *Gender Protest and Same-Sex Desire in Antebellum American Literature: Margaret Fuller, Edgar Allan Poe, Nathaniel Hawthorne, and Herman Melville*, Burlington, VT: Ashgate Publishing Co.

Halberstam, Judith [Jack] (1998) *Female Masculinity*, Durham: Duke University Press. *A Handbook for Travellers on the Continent: Being a Guide to Holland, Belgium, Prussia, Northern Germany, and the Rhine from Holland to Switzerland* (1871) 7th ed., London: John Murray.

Haskell, Francis and Nicholas Penny (1981) *Taste and the Antique: The Lure of Classical Sculpture 1500–1900*, New Haven, CT and London: Yale University Press.

James, Henry (1908) "Introduction," *The Portrait of a Lady*, vol. 1, edited by Henry James, New York: Charles Scribner's Sons: v–xxi.

—— (1986) *Roderick Hudson*, edited by Geoffrey Moore, Harmondsworth: Penguin Books. Originally published 1875.

Lodge, G. Henry, trans (1872) *History of the Ancient Art*, vols. 1 and 2, edited by Johann Joachim Winckelmann, Boston: Houghton, Mifflin and Company.

Martin, Robert K. (1978) "The 'High Felicity' of Comradeship: A New Reading of *Roderick Hudson*," *American Literary Realism*, vol. 11: 100–8.

Mendelssohn, Michèle (2003) "Homosociality and the Aesthetic in Henry James's *Roderick Hudson*," *Nineteenth-Century Literature*, vol. 57, no. 4: 512–41.

Palmer, Erastus Dow (1856) "Philosophy of the Ideal," *The Crayon*, vol. 3, no. 1: 18–20.

Pater, Walter H. (1873) *Studies in the History of the Renaissance*, London: Macmillan.

Person, Leland S. (2002) "Falling into Heterosexuality: Sculpting Male Bodies in *The Marble Faun* and *Roderick Hudson*," *Roman Holidays: American Writers and Artists in Nineteenth-Century Italy*, edited by Robert K. Martin and Leland S. Person, Iowa City: University of Iowa Press: 107–39.

Plato (1973) *Phaedrus* and *The Seventh and Eighth Letters*, translated by Walter Hamilton, London: Penguin Books.

Potts, Alex (1994) *Flesh and the Ideal: Winckelmann and the Origins of Art History*, New Haven, CT and London: Yale University Press.

Reynolds, Joshua (1997) *Discourses on Art*, edited by Robert R. Wark, Yale University Press. Originally published 1797.

Stevens, Hugh (1998) *Henry James and Sexuality*, Cambridge: Cambridge University Press.

Taylor, Bayard (1854) *Views A-Foot: Or Europe Seen with Knapsack and Staff*, New York: Putnam. Originally published 1846.

Urry, John (1990) *The Tourist Gaze: Leisure and Travel in Contemporary Societies*. London: Sage.

Willis, Nathaniel Parker (1853) *Pencillings by the Way: Written During Some Years of Residence and Travel in Europe*, Detroit: Kerr, Doughty & Lapham. Originally published 1836.

Winckelmann, Johann Joachim (1987) *Reflections on the Imitation of Greek Works in Painting and Sculpture*, translated by Elfriede Heyer and Roger C. Norton, La Salle, IL: Open Court. Originally published 1755.

—— (2006) *History of the Art of Antiquity*, translated by Harry Francis Mallgrave, Los Angeles, CA: Getty Research Institute. Originally published 1764.

Wunder, Richard P. (1991) *Hiram Powers: Vermont Sculptor, 1805–1873*, vol. 1, Newark, DE: University of Delaware Press.

5 Travelling curios in a playful spirit

Henry James's American museum[1]

Hitomi Nabae

Embedded on the pages of *The Portrait of a Lady* (1881), the following lines play out: "If I were to go to Japan next winter you would laugh at me," says Isabel Archer, to which her husband, Gilbert Osmond, responds, "I would give my little finger to go to Japan; it's one of the countries I want most to see. Can't you believe that, with my taste in lacquer?" (James *PL* 1985: 507). Neither of these two James's characters actually travels to Japan, but from this conversation we can surmise that Japan, or the "Far East" as it was often cast in James's era, was already a part of their fanciful thoughts and within reach of European and American tourist markets. The mid-nineteenth-century American literary imagination, indeed, embraced Japan as a new terrain to discover. The narrator of *Moby Dick* (1851) croons, for example, "If that double-bolted land, Japan, is ever hospitable" (Melville 1983: 911), hoping for port calls as the White Whale has been spotted off the coast of Japan. In fact, only a few years after the novel's publication, the American military commander Commodore Perry was sent to force open Japan's "double-bolted" door in 1853 and 1854, and initiate trade with the United States – an incident which quickened the curiosity of the Western world. It is not surprising, therefore, that Isabel Archer speaks of Japan while Osmond craves "lacquer."

In James's era, "Japan" acquires a double meaning, referring both to the far away and exotic place to visit and to the process of "*japan*ning," in which a fashionable and costly curio was finished in an imitation lacquer style. Although he himself never went to Japan, James's close friends, John LaFarge, Henry Adams, and another Isabel – Isabella Stewart Gardner – did around the time of the publication of *The Portrait*. They all became both avid tourists and collectors. Observing them, James must have been aware that the art world was quickly changing towards the end of the nineteenth century. It is not that James was particularly interested in "Japan"; rather, I would argue that he used "Japan" as a metaphor for both the farthest possible place from the central Europe in Isabel's imaginary world and the most curious, thus valuable, object in Osmond's, or a collector's, aesthetic world. American collectors of the Gilded Age indeed gained enough purchasing power to expand their market, which especially inspired James to look at art objects once again as things, be it merchandise or art, and urged him to consider the significance of art in the capitalistic world surrounding him, whereby the ideology of nationalism prevailed along with the imperialistic expansion. If an American should purchase a painting from a European aristocrat, does it make him a thief of someone's cultural legacy or even national identity? What significance overall do art collectors in James's fiction represent? This chapter traces the transformations of the art world James represents, from private collection to public museum, and examines James's idea of an American museum, where art objects, freed from their cultural moorings, may augment an unprecedented aesthetic experience in a new globalizing environment.

Private collections

As Sergio Perosa points out in "Henry James and Unholy Art Acquisitions," James probably had mixed feelings about Americans of the Gilded Age buying up European art. It is noteworthy that James, as a young critic, deliberately added in *Hawthorne* (1879) two items that were not in his original Notebook, "no museums, no pictures," to the list of what America lacked (James *HA* 1997: 130). He clearly viewed America as a cultural vacuum compared to Europe. However, ten years before, in 1867, when James was still in America, he wrote the following to Thomas Sergeant Perry about young America's potential to create its own culture:

> we young Americans are (without cant) men of the future . . . I look upon it as a great blessing; and I think that to be an American is an excellent preparation for culture. We have exquisite qualities as a race . . . we can deal freely with forms of civilisation not our own, can pick and choose and assimilate and in short (aesthetically etc.) claim our property wherever we find it. . . . I take it that we shall find it in our moral consciousness, our unprecedented spiritual lightness and vigour . . . my instincts quite agree with yours in looking to see something original and beautiful disengage itself from our ceaseless fermentation and turmoil.
>
> (James *CL55–72* 2006: 179–80)

James's letter was written just two years after the end of the Civil War, and yet his declaration that "to be an American is an excellent preparation for culture," is a youthful, optimistic statement.[2] In this letter, James is

concerned about his future literary career, and his reference to art appreciation and art collecting preludes his lifelong search for an aesthetic experience and his desire to build his "house of fiction," or his own imaginary
museum. Art collections depicted in his fiction, therefore, mirror James's
view of correlation between art and fiction, which simultaneously creates
an educational space for aesthetic sensibility.

James's fictional world is indeed full of art objects, which serve to demonstrate moments of aesthetic perception as well as of moral awareness of
his characters. As Viola Hopkins Winner points out, they help us look at
reality by way of readjusting our fixed ideas: "The act of perception requir-
ing preconceptions as well as an object to be perceived, he saw because
he had seen, that is, the remembered picture brought into focus for him
the otherwise blurred living scene, and, conversely, the scene reinforced
the reality of the picture" (1970: 1–2). Art objects are thus interpreted as
a means to project James's fictional world more clearly and pictorially,
enhancing a sense of reality. Adeline Tintner's *The Museum World of Henry
James* (1986) itemizes and annotates James's numerous references to art
objects and architecture. She explains that he "saw in the masterpieces of
the great museums of the world, as well as in the prized possessions of collectors, rich and suggestive analogues for what he was trying to do in his
prose" (1986: 1). James thus designed his house of fiction, and furnished
its interior just as aristocrats and collectors in Europe did with masterpieces
of the past.

James's early fiction can be called "a museum story in which both reader
and characters look at a multitude of masterpieces in the Italian art reposito-
ries" (Tintner 1986: 27). They serve as exotic tourism stories offering simu-
lated art experience overseas, but they also function as factors that drive
the ambition of characters who are possessed with the idea of collecting
and its element of control. Thus the egoistic close-minded Osmond is well
represented by his closed private collection. The scene where Isabel finds
him copying "the drawing of an antique coin" (James *PL* 1985: 444) from
a folio volume is noteworthy. While Isabel's wealth supports his expanding
collection, his world is confined within a circuit of conventions, where he
never allows a different view that may change his monomaniac world. His
copying the copy of an old coin that is no longer in circulation speaks well
for his insularity.

In *The Spoils of Poynton* (1896), James portrays a British woman, Mrs.
Gereth, who has amassed museum pieces with her husband to build a private collection. Her husband's death, however, makes her realize that she
has as a woman no inheritance right to the house full of beautiful things,
which she believes to be her property and resists handing over to her son
and his fiancé, who have no aesthetic appreciation of the house. Her only

confidante is the protagonist, an unrelated woman named Fleda Vetch, who adores Mrs. Gereth's beautiful house as well as her son, but has no legal holding over the family or the house. In the end, Poynton catches fire and the beautiful things all go up in ashes. It is as if the beautiful things themselves resisted the change of hands, the family feud over possession, or any modest desire that Fleda embraced for a small farewell gift promised by the new proprietor, Mrs. Gereth's son. The private collection thus serves as a manifestation of egoistic human drama, only to be destroyed.

The burning of Poynton could be interpreted as purification of the art works that had been secularized by the desire of humans to possess, or even as a sacrificial act to free the protagonist from her moral complexity. Poynton, however, may also demonstrate what Eric Savoy terms "archive drive." In "Aspern's Archive," he discusses the burning of letters in *The Aspern Papers*, and argues that there is something "that wills its own destruction, that is soldered to the death drive," and further, that there is "the contradictory mix of preservation and destruction" (2010: 66). A closed private collection like Poynton might be looked at similarly. If what is archived (collection) remains finite as a closed collection, there will be no circulation and no further signification, just as Osmond's act of copying a drawing of an obsolete coin suggests a vicious circle of obsolescence. An art object, collected and stored privately, thus will become like a dead corpse in a tomb. In *The Golden Bowl* (1904), the fire, or "archive drive" is described as "the aesthetic principle" that is burning in Adam Verver, another collector of James's, who is, however, conscious of his controlling and dangerously "devouring" power.

> It was all, at bottom, in him, the aesthetic principle, planted where it could burn with a cold, still flame; where it fed almost wholly on the material directly involved, on the idea (followed by appropriation) of plastic beauty, of the thing visibly perfect in its kind; where, in short, in spite of the general tendency of the "devouring element" to spread, the rest of *his spiritual furniture, modest, scattered, and tended with unconscious care, escaped the consumption that in so many cases proceeds from the undue keeping-up of profane altar-fires.* Adam Verver had in other words, learned the lesson of the senses, to the end of his own little book, without having, for a day, raised the smallest scandal in his economy at large; being in this particular not unlike those fortunate bachelors, or other gentlemen of pleasure, who so manage their entertainment of compromising company that even the austerest housekeeper, occupied and competent below-stairs, never feels obliged to give warning.
>
> (James *GB* 2011a: 589, my emphasis)

Mr. Verver's "spiritual furniture" differs from that of the preoccupied mindsets of Osmond or Mrs. Gereth. It is "modest, scattered, and tended with unconscious care," and it seems to have been the key for his successful transactions in his past business enterprise. Like "fortunate bachelors" or "gentlemen of pleasure," who are freed of complex marital or familiar relationships, he can deal with "compromising company," cleverly avoiding conflicts. Mr. Verver is not a bachelor but a widower, who had an unhappy marriage; as he used to say: "We haven't the same values" (James *GB* 2011a: 548). His wife was pleased if she was taken to "the Rue de la Paix" to shop. Her world, or "la Paix," was ironically limited to the street, "the Rue," of "costly . . . dressmakers and jewelers" (James *GB* 2011a: 550). On the other hand, Mr. Verver's world expands within. He reads poetry and follows the markers documented in "Keats's sonnet about Cortez," or "On First Looking into Chapman's Homer" that would lead to "the Golden Isles" (James *GB* 2011a: 549). Such adventure he knows is challenging as the beauty can be only viewed from atop of the "vertiginous Peak." Practical thinker that he is, he concludes that "no companion of Cortez had been a real lady" and presumes that it would have been impossible to take his wife who loves frills and ribbons on such adventure in order to show her, "as Cortez" did to his companions, "the revelation vouched" in the form of "the Golden Isles" beyond (James *GB* 2011a: 551). Stated differently, he is equipped with the requisite wealth and connoisseurship in art but not with a companion with whom he can share his vision of "the Golden Isles."

Mr. Verver proves to be not simply an avid collector with a thick wallet full of greenbacks, but a man of two minds and worlds: a practical market-oriented world that requires accurate judgements and an imaginary world that is furnished with his favourite art and literature. What he needs is a companion who can push him from behind and climb up the "vertiginous Peak." In order for James to shape Mr. Verver at once into business adventurer and art lover, as I will discuss hereafter, Isabella Stewart Gardner played an indispensable role.

The Gilded Age of American collectors

Gilded Age America brought unprecedented business growth to the United States and many wealthy businessmen who travelled to Europe started to collect art objects, including William Vanderbilt, J. P. Morgan, Henry Clay Frick, and Andrew Carnegie. These wealthy "barons" also became passionate buyers, and as the art market expanded in the United States, French and British art dealers opened branches first in New York and later throughout the country.[3] Mrs. Jack, or Isabella Stewart Gardner was a pioneer in the Gilded Age art market. She was not a businessperson herself, but through inheritance she had funds to purchase European masterpieces one after the other. As a new type of American heiress that takes on philanthropy, she inspired James's literary imagination.[4] In the 15 July 1895 entry in his *Notebooks*, James writes what he heard during a social gathering at the Borthwicks. Mrs. Gardner was the subject of the talk:

> – the deluge of people, the insane movement for movement, the ruin of thought, of life, the negation of work, of literature, the swelling roaring crowds, the "where are you going?," the age of Mrs. Jack, the figure of Mrs. Jack, the ghastly climax or denouement. It is a splendid subject – if worked round a personal action – situation.
>
> The Americans looming up – dim, vast, portentous – in their millions – like gathering waves – the barbarians of the Roman Empire.
>
> (James *NB* 1947: 207)

The future of "the age of Mrs. Jack" with "the Americans looming up" like "the barbarians of the Roman Empire" was a thought-provoking subject for James. A year after this notebook entry, in 1896, *The Spoils of Poynton* was published. It was also the year when Mrs. Gardner purchased Titian's *Rape of Europa* for an unprecedented sum for a painting. Tintner states that in this novella, James "immortali[zed]" Mrs. Jack as Mrs. Gereth. It might be said that Mrs. Gardner's collecting fury was in full swing. Although Mrs. Gardner and Mrs. Gereth share a passion for art and their names begin with "G," they turn out to be far apart in other respects. Upon the death of her husband, Mrs. Gereth was divested of her rights to the collection,[5] which flamed her desire for possession so as not to have her collection transferred to her son and his fiancé. By contrast, with the sudden death of her husband in 1898, Mrs. Gardner's passion turned to a philanthropic project of building a museum for the people of her city, Boston. From this viewpoint, Mrs. Gardner's spirit reflects that of Mr. Verver who dreams of building a museum in his hometown, an American City. *The Golden Bowl*, incidentally, was published in 1904, a year after the opening of Mrs. Gardner's museum, Fenway Court.

When it came to the actual purchasing of objects, Mrs. Gardner employed an art guide and agent, Bernard Berenson, a Lithuanian American scholar of Italian Renaissance art who was also a student of William James at Harvard. In the purchase of *The Rape of Europa*, for example, Berenson played a big role, as he had a network of local dealers. In this case, he heard from a London art dealer Otto Gunterkunst at Colnaghi about the painting. The story recounts that he originally planned to sell *The Rape of Europa* to Mrs. Warren of Boston, an acquaintance and rival of Mrs. Gardner's, and a smaller piece by Titian together with Gainsborough's *Blue Boy* to Mrs. Gardner for a better profit. But since the Duke of Westminster who was to sell *The Blue Boy* backed out, Berenson had to devise a different plan. It turned out that he persuaded Mrs. Gardner to buy *The Rape of Europa* and she grabbed it at his asking price of 20,000 pounds, even as it was priced by Gunterkunst at 18,000. Without telling Gunterkunst, Berenson pocketed the extra 2,000 pounds on top of the prearranged commission he received from the sale.[6] He certainly maneuvered Gardner's acquisition of the great Titian, which nonetheless gave her a great joy and became the central piece of her collection. Berenson wrote in his 7 June 1896 letter to Mrs. Gardner: "Why can't I be with you when *Europa* is unpacked! America is a land of wonders, but this sort of miracle it has not witnessed. Nor, I hope, seeing miracles have begun, will this be the last. I also spend much time dreaming of your Museum" (1987: 56). He kindled the fire of Mrs. Gardner's acquisitive desire. She replies: "When come *Europa?* I am feverish about it" (1987: 59).

The title of the painting, the "rape" of "Europa," fittingly speaks to Gilded Age American robber barons ravaging a European beauty. Yet, the purchasing process was not simple. Mrs. Gardner believed that Berenson was the sole agent who discovered and purchased masterpieces for her, but in actual fact, there were other dealers involved and an accumulation of commissions for her to pay. What is more curious is that Berenson's wife and colleague Mary, who was an art historian herself, had acted as his spokesperson and promoter. She avidly wrote to Mrs. Gardner a cautionary tale about how Theodore Davis, the future patron of the Metropolitan Museum, was "duped by an Italian dealer," implying that Berenson was the trustworthy agent (Johnston 2015: 74). If the Italian dealer was a swindler, so was Berenson. The art market clearly encouraged duplicity.

One might be reminded of an antique shop dealer in *The Golden Bowl*, who appears twice in the novel, and holds the key to the secret in the story. First, in an early part of the story, his antique shop in Bloomsbury provides a stage for a behind-the-scenes plot: a clandestine meeting of Charlotte and the Prince takes place there and their conversation, though in Italian, is overheard by the dealer, who is Italian and who makes notes of his customers; that is, he archives the knowledge of who's who in the market. His particular merchandise, a golden bowl, attracts Charlotte, who wants to buy it as a gift for the Prince, although he immediately discerns a flaw, a crack in the bowl. Towards the end of the novel, Maggie purchases the same bowl from the same dealer as a gift for her father, but the dealer, having discovered that her father is a renowned collector and connoisseur, rushes to her house and discloses the flaw to her ahead of time. Then he notices two photographs on the mantelpiece, which remind him of the two customers who have shown interest in the same bowl, and reveals their secret meeting to her. James knew enough about calculating and cunning antique dealers who knew how to maneuver trade and eventually affected human drama. Nonetheless, Americans outwitted British and European dealers and bought up European treasures, which all the more fascinated James and his ilk.

Mr. Verver, Charlotte, and an American museum

Building a museum in America was not a new idea for James. Already in *Roderick Hudson* (1876), as Sergio Perosa points out, Rowland Mallet fancies that it is good to "go abroad" and "purchase certain valuable specimens" of art and "then present his treasures out of hand to an American city" (James *RH* 1983: 170, qtd. in Perosa 2008: 155). In *The Golden Bowl*, an unspecified "American city" becomes a definite place name, "American City," and Rowland's fancy becomes real as Mr. Verver actually transfers his collection to the United States. His wealth is indispensable to create a substantial collection, but it is not sufficient to make his dream come true. His project, I would argue, actually sets in motion with Charlotte Stant's entrance onto the scene. Her appearance complicates the plot because of her being at once his daughter's school friend and her husband's lover, but Mr. Verver is fascinated by her and marries her. Charlotte presages a new scene of his drama, rousing his imagination once again with her piano, which leads him to a region of his mind where he has never ventured. Sharing the music, they, the player and the audience, talk without actual talking; their silence together fills the air with such intimacy "full of the echoes of talk" (James *GB* 2011a: 593).[7] Listening to her piano playing, Mr. Verver feels that "the vagueness spread itself about him like some boundless carpet, a surface delightfully soft to the pressure of his interest" (James *GB* 2011a: 593). Charlotte makes Mr. Verver look forward to his future that expands as "a boundless carpet" upon which he set foot.

Charlotte, moreover, is a director and player of her own life. She is not a mere object of his collection but a good accompanist for his museum project, a spokesperson for his inner desire. On her side, although she had to succumb to her poor status and give up marrying the Prince, she never gives up on life. She, in her own way, has a desire to survive and look up higher. Mr. Verver intuits that her tactful and flexible sociability on top of her beauty and intelligence are essential for him to make his dream of building an American museum come true. He needs a new perspective in his single-minded act of collecting in order to take action and open up his private collection to be viewed and enjoyed by others.

Adam Verver is a middle-aged man, but as his name Verver may refer to the French word for "green," and "verve" to great energy and enthusiasm, he is young in spirit.[8] The name of the country house he rents and fills with his collection is suggestively named "Fawns," or young deer, and his eyes are "youthfully, almost strangely beautiful." Though a billionaire, he has kept a modest lifestyle, wearing an old-fashioned jacket as he has adopted "a sort of sumptuary scruple" in his youth (James *GB* 2011a: 571).[9] In other words, he has not much changed in spirit from his younger days. Even his daughter Maggie seems to be in love with him.[10] His "beautiful" eyes may reflect his childlike curiosity about everything, and yet his "sumptuary" habits are proof of his strong will and disciplined lifestyle. Despite his quiet and relaxed appearance, he is a veteran American businessman whose careful and steady businesses dealings have brought him fortune: "it was art of the very inveteracy of his straw hat and his pockets, of the detachment of the attention he fixed on his slow steps from behind his secure pince-nez" (James *GB* 2011a: 955–6). With his "beautiful eyes" and his "secure pince-nez," he hunts for beautiful things, while his spectacles, an apparatus controlling his vision, keep his view adjusted to balance out the transaction.

What is unique about Verver is that despite his retirement, he still enjoys business relationships with his dealers. He seems to acquire a sense of something "real" when he has direct human contact and social connection. Interestingly, his aesthetic sense is most heightened when an appealing art object simultaneously reminds him of a person he finds attractive. Then he feels assured that they are both valuable and "real." For example, when he first lays eyes on the Prince Amerigo, who marries his daughter Maggie, he recalls a painting by Bernadino Luini.[11] The narrator adds a comment that such a comparison might appear "queer" but "[t]he note of reality . . . continued to have for him the charm and the importance of which the maximum had occasionally been reached in his great 'finds'" (James *GB* 2011a: 588). His trained business sense thus operates hand in hand with his aesthetic one. At Fawns, the country house he rents and fills with art objects, he knows Charlotte Stant to be "real" because she reminds him of his recent "find" of the beautiful "oriental tiles" that he was thinking of buying. Mr. Verver takes Charlotte to his dealer, "a certain Mr. Gutermann-Seuss of Brighton," to see the tiles together. What he enjoys is not just the blue "Damascene tiles," but also the whole conversational atmosphere that Charlotte creates with the dealer and his family. It is as if "she were herself, in her greater gaiety, her livelier curiosity and intensity, her readier, happier irony, taking him about and showing him the place" (James *GB* 2011a: 599). He has "noticed" how she can change the whole aspect of his "monomania":

> [Charlotte's] noticed the place . . . noticed everything, as from the habit of a person finding her account at any time, according to a wisdom well learned of life, in almost any "funny" impression. It really came home

to her friend [Mr. Verver] on the spot that this *free* range of observation, . . . picking out the frequent *funny* with extraordinary promptness, would verily henceforth make a different thing for him of such experiences, of the customary hunt for the possible prize, *the inquisitive play of his accepted monomania*; which different thing could probably be *a lighter and perhaps thereby a somewhat more boisterously refreshing form of sport.*

(James GB 2011a 600; emphasis added)

Mr. Verver, feeling good and "real," even paid Mr. Gutermann-Seuss's asking price without bargaining. He finds a new perspective through Charlotte's expansive and open attention, a kind of "funny," "free" and playful "sport." A beautiful woman who has lived alone, Charlotte knows her own persuasive powers, or how she can shine in a given situation. In his *Notebooks*, James writes of her as "the very figure and image of a felt interest in life, an interest as magnanimously far-spread" with a "splendid shifting sensibility" (James *NB* 1947: 77–8).[12] She is adaptable and knows how to get on with the unceasing flow of life. Mr. Verver makes two decisions: to buy the tiles and to propose to Charlotte.

Charlotte's impressing of Mr. Verver with her piano playing might be compared to a snake charmer's mesmerizing flute. His daughter, however, has a different view. It is only after her marriage to the Prince and her father's to Charlotte that Maggie comes to know about the affair between her husband and her mother-in-law. Neither she nor her father talks about it and it is never known if her father has found out about it, but Maggie imagines her father to be all-knowing and to have everything under his control, especially his wife:

> Charlotte hung behind, with emphasized attention; she stopped when her husband stopped, but at the distance of a case or two, or of whatever to her succession of objects; and the likeness of their connection would not have been wrongly figured if he had been thought of as holding in one of his pocketed hands the end of a long silken halter looped round her beautiful neck. He didn't twitch it, yet it was there; he didn't drag her, but she came.

(James GB 2011a: 926)

Maggie "translate[s]" the above scene as a message from her father saying that "yes, you see – I lead her [Charlotte] now by the neck, I lead her to her doom" (James *GB* 2011a: 927). Yet Maggie is also sympathetic. When she witnesses a scene in which Charlotte explains her father's collection to guests, she thinks her voice too painful to bear: "the high voice quavered" and it was like "the shriek of a soul in pain" (James *GB* 2011a: 929). The image of an animal emitting a pathetic cry in its cage illustrates Maggie's view of Charlotte, who is stripped of her freedom and is securely chained to Mr. Verver.[13] Nonetheless, what Mr. Verver or Charlotte thinks of the situation remains unknown. What is clear here is that Charlotte is beautifully acting out her assigned role as a spokesperson for her husband, or for his collection. What must be true, as Maggie feels, is that the whole atmosphere, a house full of collections of old things that have transferred to different hands, carries a sense of "the shame, the pity, the better knowledge, the smothered protest, the divine anguish" (James *GB* 2011a: 930).

The art objects as well as Charlotte herself silently belie the appropriateness of their current presentation, mutely testifying to their ravaged past. Even as Charlotte appears as a caged bird, just like the other collections in cabinets, her song and music are her own, and they, above all, affect Mr. Verver and trigger him to envision his museum anew. Mr. Verver is always in the background, but it is Charlotte who can articulate his view as a shrewd "*cicerone*" (James *GB* 2011a: 928). Mr. and Mrs. Verver, therefore, both find a space within Mr. Verver's collection, where they can work in concert together. Without Charlotte, Mr. Verver would neither have taken action, nor regarded it possible for him to see his imaginary "Golden Isles" in reality. Charlotte will climb up "the vertiginous Peek" with vigor, if accompanied by Mr. Verver and his wealth. It is indeed a happy transaction.

A museum: house for the homeless

Mr. and Mrs. Verver eventually come to say farewell to Portland Place, the house of Maggie, the Prince, and the Principino. On the day of their departure, Maggie has an impression that her father and mother-in-law are creating a new situation: "Mr. and Mrs. Verver were making the occasion easy. They were somehow conjoined in it, conjoined for a present effect as Maggie had absolutely never yet seen them" (James *GB* 2011a: 974). In this scene, father and daughter take a last look at the pieces they purchased together, as well as at Mrs. Verver and the Prince, who are also objects of their attention: they have fallen "into the splendid effect and the general harmony" and are "fairly 'placed' themselves, however unwittingly, as high expressions of the kind of human furniture required aesthetically by such a scene" (James *GB* 2011a: 976). This description may indeed imply that they are reduced to mere objects, and in fact, the narrator adds that they might appear "as concrete attestations of a rare power of purchase." Mr. Verver, a man of few words, furthermore tells Maggie with some contentment, "*Le compte y est*. You've got some good things" (James *GB* 2011a: 976). Without his wealth, both the animate and inanimate things in his view could not have been amassed. Yet, the "human furniture" does not necessarily mean that Amerigo and Charlotte are bought as merchandise; they might also signify a different aspect in which to represent humans by the roles they play in certain settings, like "furniture" in a room. Both Amerigo and Charlotte are homeless and have no place to which they belong. Amerigo is by pedigree an Italian prince, but his property in Italy crumbled away, and Charlotte, with her beauty and intelligence, is a lone cosmopolitan in the world without home or money. Neither their family names nor nationalities are sufficient to certify their identity in the globalizing capitalist world. Mr. Verver's wealth can only create a museum-like space for them to draw out their intrinsic worth – their grace, beauty and intelligence.[14]

Just as the human figures in James's works represent floating signifiers, losing ground to any identity, so are the art objects. James's final novel originally written as a play in 1907, *The Outcry* (1911), offers, to quote the *Times Literary Supplement*, "a positively exciting plot" (qtd. in Strouse 2002); it is played out as a comedy with the British raising an "outcry" at an American who tries to buy their treasures, or Britain's "art-wealth" (James *O* 2011b: 53). The plot was timely for it was in 1909 when Henry Clay Frick attempted to buy Hans Holbein the Younger's *The Duchess of Milan* and the British impeded the purchase by raising $350,000 to buy it for the National Gallery instead. In James's telling, an American Breckenridge Bender (whose initials recall Bernard Berenson)[15] is referred to as a "money monster" or "dreadful rich thing" and is one of "such a conquering horde as invaded the old civilization, only armed now with huge chequebooks instead of with spears and battle-axes" (James *O* 2011b: 1059). He is after a portrait by Sir Joshua Reynolds which hangs in Lord Theign's country house, Dedborough, whose name clearly indicates that it is not only Americans but also the British that are made fun of. The Dedborough is corrupted as Lord Theign's older daughter is in a great debt from playing cards, and, rather than selling Sir Joshua, he thinks of marrying away his second and far more intelligent daughter Grace to a repugnant Lord John, whose mother the elder sister is indebted to. The daughter is thus treated as a valuable asset, though less so than the painting. The story nonetheless ends happily as Lord Theign decides to donate his paintings to the National Gallery, thereby identifying them as British national treasures, and consequently saving them from ravaging Americans.

The irony in *The Outcry*, moreover, is that the British owners of the paintings do not really know the worth of their collection, neither the authorship and provenance, nor their assessed value in the art market. In this regard, the introduction of a new generation of art historians is noteworthy. Mr. Hugh, a nationalist himself, is a young art historian with whom Grace is in love. As he had a hunch that one of Lord Theign's paintings is wrongly identified, he decides to ask the opinion of "an expert" in Italian Renaissance art, a Mr. Pappendick. Mr. Hugh travels to Brussels to invite the expert to England to inspect the case where his theory is proven. Jean Strouse points out that James was aware of the new trend of art history: "James alludes here to the German-educated Italian art historian Giovanni Morelli (1816–1891), whose method of searching for significant, revealing particulars in works of art had helped substitute comparative procedures for subjective feeling in the 'science' of attribution – and whose disciples included Bernard Berenson, Gustavo Frizzoni, and Jean-Paul Richter" (2002). Mr. Hugh is excited to discover the true identity of the painting.

The new generation of experts, therefore, is rewriting art history. In the early 1900s, Mary Berenson delivered lectures on "The New Art Criticism" to raise the levels of American taste. In the lectures that she gave at Bryn Mawr in 1904, she emphasized "the scientific method from Giovanni Morelli," "the historical method from Gaetano Milanesi," "the Psychological aspect from William James," and "the aesthetic approach from Walter Pater" (Johnston 2015: 79).[16] Mary unveils how "the new art criticism" changes the list of "sacred pictures." Judgement by a shifting panel of critics, therefore, rewrites the identities of art objects whose values no longer rely on the ownership, be they of an aristocratic family or a nation, but on a comparative scientific method which, of course, inevitably affects market value. This dynamic then explains why, at the end of *The Outcry*, Mr. Bender shifts his interest to the newly discovered (but old) painting, since, for rarity, its "pecuniary" value on the market will rise (James *O* 2011b: 1032). James thus subtly portrays how the evaluation of new scientific systems is linked with the art market. Further, if the attributes of art objects are subject to change according to the new system of knowledge, as described in James's story, it means that what we assume are essential values attached to them do not really exist.

The Outcry questions the significance of art objects in terms of ownership and value. The only person aware of this contingency is Grace, who is treated as an exchangeable asset, and seeks freedom. She believes in Mr. Hugh's hypothesis and his scientific method, but also points out his nationalistic bias. When he calls plundering Americans "awful," she retorts to him that they, the Britons, were also "awful" because their art objects were similarly stolen from somewhere (James *O* 2011b: 1127). Art objects are immune and they bear imposed values and identities. They are free signifiers whose identities can be negotiated according to new definitions and settings, just as a piece of furniture gains meaning according to the surrounding interior of a house.

If art objects may acquire new value detached from emotional, familiar and national identities, so is the case of humans. James's use of "human furniture" arguably is not derogatory. Humans, like objects, were likely to gain meaning according to the circumstances, or the roles they play, in a given situation in the coming age of capitalistic and imperialistic world. Mr. Verver's American museum then offers a space for a new set of values to be gathered and amalgamated. His outlook ascribes meaning to the so-called homeless, be they things or humans.

The future for travelling curios

Although James might have described Mrs. Gardner as "one of the trans-atlantic 'barbarians' over-ruling Europe, carrying off shiploads of spoils" (Edel 1977 vol. 1: 579), he was enthralled to hear that she opened a museum, Fenway Court, to the public and put *The Rape of Europa* on view in 1903. Americans might be "robber barons," but Mrs. Gardner's daring decision to share her experience with the public (Figure 5.1) struck James as "admirable." He wrote to Paul Bourget about her "*Palais-musée*":

> [Mrs. Gardner's museum] is a really great creation. Her acquisitions during the last ten years have been magnificent; her arrangement and administration of them are admirable, and her spirit soars higher still. Her spirit is immense, and proof against time and fate. It has greatly "improved" her in every way to have done a thing of so much interest and importance – and to have had to do it with such almost unaided courage and intelligence and energy. She has become really a great little personage.
>
> (James *Letters* 1987 vol. 4: 389)

In *The American Scene*, James writes about the Metropolitan Museum, where J. P. Morgan, a financier and businessman outfitted with a degree in art history from a German university, had just become the president when James was visiting. Therein, James smells money. But at the same time, he feels the "reiterated sacrifice of pecuniary profit" that makes him imagine behind-the-scene stories of "the harshness or the sadness, the pang" felt in the past. However, he leaves his lamentations behind and quickly adjusts his viewpoint to the museum's "advantage to the spirit, not to the pocket," naming three points:

> first, perhaps, the scale on which, in the past, bewildering tribute has flowed in; second, the scale on which it must absolutely now flow out; and third, the presumption created by the vivacity of these two

movements for a really fertilizing stir of the ground – he sees the whole place as the field of a drama the nearer view of the future course of which he shall be sorry to lose.

(James *AS* 1993: 513)

At the museum, or "a place of art" (James *AS* 1993: 512), James points to the past "flowing in," the present "flowing out," and the dynamic torrent of "these two movements" to create a new "ground" for a "future course." James repeats the word "education" and opines how it is "seated" in the museum's "marble halls" to "issue her instructions without regard to cost" (James *AS* 1993: 513). James is aware that "the *exquisite* things" can be "invidious" and "cruel" from a personal point of view, but they "take on a high benignity as soon as the values concerned become values mainly for the mind" (James *AS* 1993: 514). The museum offers a space for the mind to open up. He concludes his account of the Metropolitan Museum with the following statement: "The Museum, in short, was going to be great, and in the geniality of the life to come such sacrifices, though resembling those of the funeral-pile of Sardanapalus, dwindled to nothing" (James *AS* 1993: 514).

Figure 5.1 Visitors viewing *The Rape of Europa* (Titian, 1562), Titian Room at the Isabella Stewart Gardner Museum. Digital photograph by Hitomi Nabae, 2016.

When we think of museums today, they more or less serve the role of a theme park – there must be elements of sport, surprise, and shared experience, not to mention educational content of history and culture. The art market is increasingly making profit, but do not the art objects themselves refuse to be strictly defined by a "pecuniary" market value? Strictly speaking, their authorship fluctuates as they change hands and they tell different stories according to the arrangement in which they are set – an exhibition according to classified museum catalogues or featured exhibitions overseas, for example. An element of sport and fun is, as I have argued, what Mr. Verver learns from Charlotte. In Maggie's view, she represents "the shame, the pity, the better knowledge, the smothered protest, the divine anguish" (James *GB* 2011a: 930), or history itself. Contrary to such thinking, however, when she leads a group of guests around Mr. Verver's collection, Charlotte is described as a determined and articulate but also spontaneously improvising *cicerone*. She acts her role perfectly and in fact Mr. Verver's museum needs a guide like her who is always aware of her position in the fluctuating circumstances of the world and is meaningful and "funny" as a living Baedeker.

Both Isabel and Osmond desired to travel to other cultural worlds, such as Japan. Mrs. Gereth regarded her collection finite and her taste the standard of appreciation. Mr. Verver needed to travel to acquire art objects in order to bring them to his country to create an aesthetic space to raise the moral of his fellow citizens. His museum pieces unfold a new story, uprooted and flowing in the stream of time in a playful spirit. They will also be shared more happily with the public. As we witness today, museum pieces travel overseas for special exhibitions, even to the Far East, to Japan – the "drama" James imagined seems to be projected on the travelling curios of world museums that are continuously re-selected and re-arranged in a new multicultural and national settings. I might also add that, a hundred years after James's death today, the plasticity of a new museum envisioned in James's fiction still challenges the ideas of ownership and identity, raising issues such as repatriation or repossession of art objects and exotic curios to their native cultures.

Notes

1 The original version of my chapter was presented at the 28th American Literature Association Conference held in Boston, 25–28 May 2017, under the title, "Ideas for a Museum Traveling Curios and Preservation of Culture in Late Henry James," in a panel, " 'If I were to go to Japan': Theory and Practice of Travel in Henry James and Beyond" moderated by Mirosława Buchholtz. This is part of my project "Umi wo wataru Katari: H. James to L. Hearn [Traveling Narrative in Henry James and Lafcadio Hearn]" supported by JSPS KAKENHI Grant Number JP16K0298.

2 Interestingly, Inge Reist began her keynote lecture, "What's Mine Is Yours: Private Collectors and Public Patronage in the United States" at the 2016 conference *Private Collecting and Public Display* also with this quotation.

3 The European branch offices encouraged the art market in the United States but it was not until the 1880s that large sales of works of art regularly took place. Michaël Vittero makes a point that "The pictorial production of the Gilded Age, collected by the American elite, and related to investment and philanthropy, remains relatively neglected." See "To Collect and Conquer: American Collections in the Gilded Age" (2013).

4 Isabella Stewart was born in New York City in 1840 as the daughter of David Stewart, who made a fortune in Irish linen and later mining investments. She married her friend's brother, Jack Gardner, whose family made a fortune by Chinese trade. When her father died in 1891, she inherited an estate valued at $1.75 million. The following year she bought Johannes Vermeer's *The Concert* at the Paris auction. The Gardners travelled around the world and started collecting art works with a museum in their mind. Mr. Gardner, however, died suddenly of a stroke in 1898. See *The Isabella Stewart Gardner Museum* (Goldfarb 1995: 3–18).

5 The idea for *The Golden Bowl* can be tracked back to the 28 November 1892 entry in his *Notebooks* with references to the father and daughter relationship and marriages. But the actual writing took place in the years 1903–1904. He had just sent his manuscript to Scribner's when he sailed for America in August 1905. See Edel 1977, vol. 2: 531.

6 See Charles FitzRoy (2015) Chapter 7, "Isabella Stewart Gardner, Bernard Berenson and the Creation of her Museum." The painting cost her approximately $100,000, which is about $2,743,802 today.

7 The first masterpiece Mrs. Gardner purchased was Johannes Vermeer's *The Concert*, which was stolen in 1990 and has been missing since.

8 Colm Tóibín refers to James's 22 May 1892 notebook entry as the first rough sketch of Mr. Verver: "Another man – not a Newman, but more completely civilized, large, rich, complete, but strongly characterized, but essentially a *product*. Get the action – the action in which to launch him – it should be a big one I have not difficulty in *seeing* the figure – it *comes*, as I look at it" (James 1947: 125, qtd. in Tóibín 2017: 32).

9 Caroline G. Mercer (1967) quotes these passages in her argument on Adam Verver as a "Yankee Businessman."

10 Maggie has accompanied her father in his search of art objects and shared his views. Her view changes through her marriage and the knowledge of her husband's duplicity. Although she was always with her father when he bought art objects, she does not have an actual role to play in Mr. Verver's museum in American City. Rather, she consciously takes up her role as wife and mother, and her house at Portland Place will presumably become an ideal beautiful space for her family.

11 When he was first introduced to the Prince, his future son-in-law, Mr. Verver knew that he was real: he discerns "marks and signs" of "the high authenticities" (James *GB* 2011a: 549).

12 In one of very few readings with a focus on Charlotte Stant, Jean Kimball refers to this scene as one that depicts Charlotte as a heroine resembling James's cousin Minny Temple, whom he remembered as a "restless spirit, the finest reckless impatience." See Kimball (1957).

13 Susan Griffin persuasively traces the depiction of Charlotte as a caged bird, or as a beast. Griffin implies that "Maggie desires a state of nature, free from the prisonlike structures of civilization" (1991: 74). See *Henry James and Historical Eye*.

14 In this sense, another great "find," Prince Amerigo, is happily placed at Portland Place with his family, Maggie and the Principino. An international couple with a son in a beautiful house is Mr. Verver's another creative achievement on the other side of the Atlantic.

15 Tintner argues that Mr. Bender, "the billionaire with the checkbook always in hand, ready to buy only the most expensive pictures, has clearly been modeled on [J. Piermont] Morgan" (1986: 227).

16 James gave his Bryn Mawr lecture, "The Questions of Our Speech," a year later in June 1905. It is most likely that he had read Mary Berenson's articles or heard about her from Mrs. Gardner. She was the key figure in the art market for American millionaire buyers. See Johnston (2015).

Bibliography

Berenson, Bernard and Isabella Stewart Gardner (1987) *The Letters of Bernard Berenson and Isabella Stewart Gardner 1887–1924*, edited and annotated by Rollin van N. Hadley. Boston: Isabella Stewart Gardner Museum.

Edel, Leon (1977) *The Life of Henry James*, vols. 1 and 2, Harmondsworth: Penguin Books.

FitzRoy, Charles (2015) *The Rape of Europa: The Intriguing History of Titian's Masterpiece*, Kindle edn., Bloomsbury: Continuum.

Goldfarb, Hilliard T. (1995) *The Isabella Stewart Gardner Museum: A Companion Guide and History*, New Haven, CT and London: Yale University Press.

Griffin, Susan (1991) *Henry James and Historical Eye: The Texture of the Visual in Late Henry James*, Boston: Northeastern University Press.

James, Henry (1947) *The Notebooks of Henry James*, edited by F. O. Matthiessen and Kenneth B. Murdock, Oxford: Oxford University Press.

——— (1983) *Roderick Hudson, Henry James Novels 1871–1880*, edited by T. Stafford, New York: Library of America: 163–512. Originally published 1875.

——— (1984) *The Letters of Henry James*, vol. 4, edited by Leon Edel. Cambridge, MA: Harvard University Press.

——— (1985) *The Portrait of a Lady, Henry James: Novels 1881–1886*, edited by William Stafford and New York: Library of America: 191–800. Originally published 1881.

——— (1993) *The American Scene, Henry James: Collected Travel Writings*, annotated by Richard Howard, New York: Library of America: 351–736. Originally published 1907.

——— (1997) *Hawthorne*, Ithaca, NY: Cornel University Press. Originally published 1879.

——— (2003) *The Spoils of Poynton, Henry James: Novels: 1896–1899*, edited by Myra Jehlen, New York: Library of America: 211–394. Originally published 1896.

—— (2006) *The Complete Letters of Henry James 1855–1872*, vol. 1, edited by Pierre A. Walker and Greg W. Zacharias, Lincoln and London: University of Nebraska Press.

—— (2011a) *The Golden Bowl, Henry James: Novels 1903–1911*, edited by Ross Posnock, New York: Library of America: 431–982. Originally published 1904.

—— (2011b) *The Outcry, Henry James: Novels 1903–1911*, edited by Ross Posnock, New York: Library of America: 983–1136. Originally published 1911.

Johnston, Tiffany (2015) "Mary Berenson and the Cultivation of American Collectors," *A Market for Merchant Painters: Collecting Italian Renaissance Paintings in America*, edited by Inge Reist, University Park, PA: Pennsylvania State University Press: 72–81.

Kimball, Jean (1957) "Henry James's Last Portrait of a Lady: Charlotte Stant in *The Golden Bowl*," *American Literature*, vol. 28, no. 4: 229–68.

Melville, Herman (1983) *Moby-Dick. Melville: Redburn White-Jacket, Moby-Dick*, edited by G. Thomas Tanselle, New York: Library of America.

Mercer, Caroline G. (1967) "Adam Verver, Yankee Businessman," *Nineteenth-Century Fiction*, vol. 22, no. 3: 251–69.

Perosa, Sergio (2008) "Henry James and Unholy Art Acquisitions." *The Cambridge Quarterly*, vol. 37, no. 1: 150–63.

Reist, Inge (2017) "What's Mine Is Yours: Private Collectors and Public Patronage in the United States," *YouTube*, uploaded by Dumbarton Oaks, 26 June 2017, www.youtube.com/watch?v=w3UHMLkfTlk. Accessed 8 May 2017.

Savoy, Eric (2010) "Aspern's Archive," *The Henry James Review*, vol. 31, no. 1, Winter: 61–7.

Strouse, Jean (2002) "James's Last Bow," *The New York Review of Books*, 25 April 2002, www.nybooks.com/articles/2002/04/25/jamess-last-bow/. Accessed 8 May 2017.

Tintner, Adeline (1986) *The Museum World of Henry James*. Ann Arbor, MI: UMI Research Press.

Tóibín, Colm (2017) "Henry James: Shadow and Substance," *Henry James and American Painters*, University Park, PA: Pennsylvania State University Press/ New York: Morgan Library &Museum: 1–48.

Vittero, Michaël (2013) "To Collect and Conquer: American Collections in the Gilded Age," *Transatlantica: American Studies Journal*, vol. 1: 1–11. http://transatlantica.revues.org/6492

Winner, Viola Hopkins (1970) *Henry James and Visual Arts*, Charlottesville, VA: University of Virginia Press.

6   Back in "the terrible city"

Henry James and his characters in search of the past and a less polarized future

Urszula Gołębiowska

Henry James's characters are strangely mobile – they travel, most often but not only, from America to Europe and back, allowing the writer's novels and tales to explore various implications of their confrontations with foreign places and cultures. Whether inscribed in the writer's "international theme" or not, travel in his works is invariably connected with the notion of experience – a crucial category which has acquired a broad significance in James's work. In the often-quoted fragment of the 1908 preface to *The Princess Casamassima* (1886) James explains that "[e]xperience . . . is our apprehension and our measure of what happens to us as social creatures" (James 1962: 64–5). While the word "apprehension" suggests that perceptions play an important role in experience, the addition of measure indicates that experience is not limited to receiving impressions, but involves an attempt at understanding their meaning. For James then, experience is not just a series of sensual data registered in the consciousness, but what individuals make of those impressions and sensations, which applies to the experience of travel both in the writer's travelogues and fictions. As early as in 1873 James remarked in a letter to his brother William that it is not the recording of the "picturesque" that interests him. He added that the "*keen* love and observation of the picturesque is ebbing away from me as I grow older, and I doubt whether a year or two hence I shall have it in me to describe houses and mountains, or even cathedrals and pictures. I don't know whether I shall do anything better, but I shall have been spoiled for this" (James *CL72–76* 2008: 294). Consequently, rather than merely recording visual impressions, James's travel writings demonstrate an effort at extracting meaning from the sights visited, mining perceptions for associations, connections, and echoes of the past. What emerges is a complex interplay of surface and depth, of present impressions and memory, of consciousness and external reality, confirming that "relations stop nowhere" (James Preface to *RH* 1986: 260) and "there is no such thing as an unrelated fact" (James *AS* 1994: 231).

Relations and connections abound in James's twentieth-century texts which stage long-term expatriates' visits to America, even though their encounters with the land do not seem at first productive of rich associations or insights. In *The American Scene* (1907), a travelogue inspired by James's 1904–1905 return visit to America after a twenty-year absence, the writer often bemoans the inherent emptiness and uniformity of the American scene, at the same time ironically subverting the conviction, foundational for his project, that a critically disposed and diligent observer should be able to extract a synthetic meaning from the observed reality:

> To be critically, or as we have been fond of calling it, analytically, minded – over and beyond an inherent love of the general many-coloured picture of things – is to be subject to the superstition that objects and places, coherently grouped, disposed for human use and addressed to it, must have a sense of their own, a mystic meaning proper to themselves to give out: to give out, that is to the participant at once so interested and so detached as to be moved to a report of the matter. That perverse person is obliged to take it for a working theory that the essence of almost any settled aspect of anything may be extracted by the chemistry of criticism, and may give us its right name, its formula, for convenient use.
>
> (James *AS* 1994: 202)

By calling the belief underlying analytical ventures a "superstition" or a "working theory" and by referring to the critic as "that perverse person," the autobiographical narrator of *The American Scene* seemingly undermines the very premise informing the travelogue, ironically balancing the mastery implicit in the critical intention with the awareness of the illusory essence assumed to reside in things and phenomena. Nevertheless, what follows is an articulation of the importance of the sense-making activity. Irrespective of the difficulty of extraction due to the emptiness or incoherence of a scene, considerable effort must be expended to produce meanings:

> From the moment the critic finds himself sighing, to save trouble in a difficult case, that the cluster of appearances can *have* no sense, from that moment he begins . . . to go to pieces; it being the prime business and the high honour of the painter of life always to *make* a sense – and to make it most in proportion as the immediate aspects are loose or confused.
>
> (James *AS* 1994: 202)

The desire to extract or produce meaning and value are in evidence on the pages of *The American Scene*, even if, at times, the encountered vacuity, blandness, and incoherence are in themselves expressive, making the writer "renounce . . . the subtle effort to 'read' a sense into senseless appearances about me" (James *AS* 1994: 288). It is not only the epistemological difficulty of understanding the incoherent American scene that interferes with the desire to make sense of the encounter. As this chapter will show, the reengagements with America in James's travelogue and the short stories "The Jolly Corner" (1908) and "A Round of Visits" (1910) demonstrate that the challenge of revisiting the long-lost home is intimately connected with the past that cannot be comfortably revisited in historic and personal landmarks. The forgotten or repressed past needs to be engaged with to make intelligible the present moment and experience.

What illuminates the struggles of James's returnees in America is Salman Rushdie's claim that "the past is a country from which we have all emigrated" (1991: 12). By conflating time and place, the statement suggests that expatriate, transnational individuals have not only abandoned a place but left behind a specific moment, to which it is impossible to return. The transformative passage of time makes it impossible to recapture past experience in *The American Scene* – much has been written about James's understanding of the impact of the accelerated process of modernity, how it "revokes the authority of the past through new economies of scale and the infusion of difference" (Graham 2010: 316). As the autobiographical narrator of *The American Scene* travels through the United States, trying to identify the contemporary American character and searching for traces of the past, the text repeatedly describes shocking transformations that he encounters.

New York is by far the most frequent site of loss mourned as well as time recaptured "at every turn, in sights, sounds, smells, even in the chaos of confusion and change" (James *AS* 1994: 5). What becomes instantly apparent is the radical character of the change that has transformed the city of James's childhood into the early twentieth-century metropolis, rendering the interpretation of the observed reality similar to "the spelling out of foreign sentences of which one knows but half the words" (James *AS* 1994: 5). The trope of disrupted readability captures the confrontation with the city profoundly altered by the recent industrialization, building boom, and mass immigration. The rapid change, underscored by the native orientation towards the future, frustrates the narrator's attempts to encounter the past as historic or personal landmarks have been either obscured from view by new buildings or mercilessly demolished. The absence of James's birthplace in Washington Square, which has given way to an impersonal skyscraper, leaves him with the trauma of "having been amputated of half my history" (James *AS* 1994: 71). The famous Trinity Church is fortunately still there, yet almost obliterated by the recently erected towers – products of a building boom unrestrained by a sense of the past or respect for cultural legacy.

The church's "smothered visibility" (James *AS* 1994: 63) inspires a reflection on the skyscrapers as expressive of the American commercial spirit and representing "the expensively provisional," serving immediate purposes as "triumphant payers of dividends" (James *AS* 1994: 60).

Effected by modernity, the defamiliarization of reality and the alienation of the subject facing the unreal world complicate both the project of revisiting the past and that of understanding the present experience. Modernity in *The American Scene* emerges as a force unleashed and unchecked, infusing New York with a self-sustaining power "detached from any human agency" and severed from the past (Savoy 2010: 360). To the bewildered spectator the city appears like a cross between a monstrous organism and a self-perpetuating mechanical construction. Consistent with this ambivalent vision, the metaphors employed to represent New York are informed by the sense of the city and its buildings as animated either by a life force or by a mechanism (Savoy 2010: 360). On the one hand, New York appears like "the monster [that] grows and grows, flinging abroad its loose limbs" or "the monstrous organism," on the other, it seems propelled by "an enormous system of steam-shuttles or electric bobbins" (James *AS* 1994: 59). Eventually, the mechanical aspect is expected to prevail, the future city imagined as a complex web, a "colossal set of clockworks, some steel-souled machine-room of brandished arms and hammering fists and opening and closing jaws" (James *AS* 1994: 59). The "universal *applied* passion" (James *AS* 1994: 59) animating the city is an impersonal force that also operates in its parts, the tall buildings, the "huge constructed and compressed communities, throbbing, through its myriad arteries and pores, with a single passion, . . . as a complicated watch throbs with the one purpose of telling you the hour and the minute" (James *AS* 1994: 64). It is the commercial passion that mobilizes the immense power apparent in the skyscrapers, those "monsters of the mere market," effecting an abrupt break with the past, the break that complicates the effort to derive meaning from the encounter with the American scene (James *AS* 1994: 63).

Even though Boston has been affected to a lesser extent than New York by rapid modernization, it is nevertheless a stage of a failure to connect with the past – it involves another witness to James's personal history, the house where he had spent two years "of far-away youth" (James *AS* 1994: 170). The demolition of the building during James's stay in America inspires a reflection on the sudden disappearance of a part of his biography. Still standing on the writer's first visit to Boston, the house has been erased before his return to the city:

> I had been present, by the oddest hazard, at the very last moments of the victim in whom I was most interested; the act of obliteration had

been breathlessly swift. . . . It was as if the bottom had fallen out of one's biography, and one plunged backward into space without meeting anything.

(James *AS* 1994: 170)

It is thus the sense of "the rupture" that the narrator-James carries from the scene, the absence of another landmark of his personal history rendering the American part of his biography a gaping void (James *AS* 1994: 171). This lack of continuity also pervades the return to the Boston Athenaeum – a famous library cum art gallery – as this "temple of culture," like the Trinity Church in New York, has been overshadowed by a "detestable tall building" (James *AS* 1994: 173). The trope of personification employed here to represent the skyscrapers as school bullies menacing a little studious boy and mocking his pretensions to exquisiteness recurs in *The American Scene* to highlight the spectral character of the past (James *AS* 1994: 173). In Cambridge, at least, the ghosts can still be felt, for "ghosts belong only to places and suffer and perish with them" (James *AS* 1994: 180). Yet, the invoked presence of two nineteenth-century poets James Russell Lowell and Henry Wadsworth Longfellow makes the writer muse about another conspicuous loss – the absence of "literary interest or curiosity" in contemporary America (James *AS* 1994: 54). The ghostly pair beside him, the narrator visits Fresh Pond, where he used to take walks with friends, only to find that "there was practically no Fresh Pond any more," the quiet place dominated by recent additions, particularly by a "gregarious" country club (James *AS* 1994: 56). Fresh Pond is "almost angrily missed" as another lost place where James had hoped to recover "some echo of the dreams of youth, the titles of tales, the community of friendship" (James *AS* 1994: 56).

James's nostalgia, evident in the descriptions of failed encounters with important sites of personal memory, is not simply a sentimental desire to revisit an idealized lost home, but a need to engage with and understand the past and the present. While nostalgia may be defined as a "longing for a home that no longer exists or has never existed," what appears to be a longing for a place is actually, as earlier noted, a "yearning for a different time," which is hoped to be revisited, like a place (Boym 2007: 7). What James's nostalgia involves is a desire for a creative dialogue between past and present that could foster continuity by connecting private memory to the contemporary cultural reality. If invoking memory often serves the purpose of exposing the present moment as corrupted by the effects of modernization, it does not mean that nostalgia is necessarily anti-modern; as Svetlana Boym argues, it may be "off-modern," offering a critique of the modern pursuit of and fascination with newness, which is evident in James's focus on the erasure of history witnessed, among other places, in

New York, Boston, and Cambridge. The forgetfulness, or repression of the past, in contemporary America results in a culture impoverished by rapid modernization and material progress. The narrator is appalled by the conspicuous "presentism," by the whole culture developing without the benefit of the "troublesome history" or "the long, the immitigable process of time" and taking a short-cut rather than a "roundabout experience" (James *AS* 1994: 13, 14). It is money that makes the short-cut possible, allowing people not to bother with cumbersome traditions or manners, which is why most Americans wish above all "[t]o make so much money that you won't, that you don't 'mind,' don't mind anything" (James *AS* 1994: 176). James's critique, however, is not motivated by excessive hatred of the present, it is rather a "reflective" form of nostalgia, meditating on a sense of personal and cultural loss. In contrast to "restorative" nostalgia which aims at a "transhistorical reconstruction of the lost home," its reflective counterpart values fragments of memory and temporalizes space, engaging in both longing and critical thinking (Boym 2007: 15–16).

The critique of negative aspects of American culture, occasioned by the nostalgic ventures into the past, results in a polarized vision of reality evident in the frequently emphasized opposition between the valorized past and the vulgar present, between Europe and America, the spiritual and the material. On the personal level, this polarization corresponds with a sense of separation and a lack of continuity, which impedes the project of understanding the returnee's experience. This feeling gives way to a different engagement with the present reality as soon as the "repentant absentee" submits to the scene, renouncing the impulse to analyse and judge (James *AS* 1994: 6). The transition from criticism to transformed perception is evident in the response to the social scene at the Waldorf-Astoria hotel in New York. What initially strikes the narrator is the enviable "perfect human felicity" (James *AS* 1994: 81) reigning in the hotel, where hundreds of people "sit under palms and by fountains," manifestly deriving pleasure from the performance of those collective "rites" (James *AS* 1994: 81). The whole scene appears as if orchestrated by some invisible but pervasive master-spirit of management, inspiring and satisfying ever new desires and instincts. Again, the resulting uniformity of human types controlled by the coercive power of the market provokes incisive comments, which become, however, interrupted by the narrator's momentary surrender to the appeal of the place. As soon as the critical impulse relaxes, the hotel appears like a "golden blur," disabling the compulsion to analyse and interpret and allowing the narrator to yield to the attraction of this "paradise peopled with unmistakable American shapes" (James *AS* 1994: 81). When the narrator finds in himself the capacity for enjoyment, which he shares with his compatriots, the opposition between the self and the other or the self and reality is momentarily dissolved. This and other moments of mastery renounced qualify previous criticism, introducing a possibility for a less polarized vision of the scene and a different understanding of experience, which reappear in the subsequent short fictions inspired by James's visit to America.

The issues of the importance of the past and the insufficiency of criticism for making sense of the complex reality recur in the short fictions written after *The American Scene*. Initially, a critical disposition towards the revisited homeland marks the response of the nostalgic protagonists of "The Jolly Corner" and "A Round of Visits," even though they do not aspire, like the "restless analyst" of the travelogue, to detect in or read into the scene the much sought-after meanings. Criticism is implicit in the returnees' reactions to America, their nostalgia not involving a conscious reflection but an unconscious desire to recapture the past. In the short fictions, the invoked past returns in uncanny forms, embodied as a human or a ghostly other. According to Eric Savoy, the return of an American protagonist to his native country after a long expatriation may be "usefully characterized as a return of the repressed and the repudiated – what Spencer Brydon in 'The Jolly Corner' understands as 'all the old baffled forsworn possibilities' that are shadowed forth from . . . the past" (Savoy 1999b: 163). On this reading, the engagement with the past, which is at the centre of "The Jolly Corner," takes the form of trying not so much to find traces of the past in the present, but to encounter a potential, unrealized American self. In the story, Spencer Brydon, a repatriated American, returns to his native New York after a thirty-three-year absence to find himself unexpectedly involved in business as well as exploring his hypothetical American past. Brydon's initial reaction to New York resembles the narrator's response in *The American Scene:* "the difference, the newnesses, the queernesses, above all the bignesses . . . assaulted his vision wherever he looked" (James JC 2001: 550). Appalled by the incalculable material and social transformations, he finds himself, nevertheless, surprisingly well-adapted to the business aspect of the scene – while supervising the renovation of the apartment building he inherited, he shows an unsuspected "capacity for business and a sense for construction" (James JC 2001: 551). At nights, however, Brydon is compelled to haunt the family house on the "jolly corner," which he keeps unaltered for sentimental reasons. His obsessive visits are, however, not motivated by the memory of events and family members who had lived and died there, but by a desire to find out "what he personally might have been, how he might have led his life and 'turned out'" if he had stayed in America (James JC 2001: 557). The answer is expected to be provided by an encounter with his spectral self which, as Brydon senses, resides in the house.

The eventual confrontation with the apparition enacts both Brydon's haunting and being haunted by the past. Driven by an epistemological obsession he shares with numerous Jamesian protagonists, Brydon feels compelled to solve the riddle of his hypothetical American self. In his pursuit of the ghostly other, Brydon acts as a hunter, "stalking" and feeling sorry for the "poor hard-pressed alter ego" (James JC 2001: 562). The situation changes with a sudden recognition of a strange reversal, of himself being "definitely followed, tracked at a distance . . . kept in sight while remaining . . . sightless" (James JC 2001: 563). The externalized identity he has been trying to hunt down and fix, fixes him instead – in the final confrontation Brydon collapses under the double's powerful gaze. The figure that represents his possible American self, a man in evening dress with two fingers missing on one of his hands, has been interpreted as that of a ruthless businessman ravaged by cruel business dealings. According to this reading, the fact that Brydon cannot fully acknowledge and recognize the double as part of himself – "the bared identity was too hideous" – signifies a disavowal of the qualities which remain latent in his nature (James JC 2001: 571). By contrast, in Savoy's reading, Brydon represents a "gay subject who obsesses about his foreclosed heterosexual past." His reunion in America with Alice Staverton, a longtime friend, stirs "the old baffled foresworn possibilities" – Brydon's "repressed heteronormative desire," generating the ghostly double (Savoy 1999a: 8–10). The trajectory of the confrontation and the subsequent rejection of the abject other suggest a fear of the closeted identity as Brydon's double embodies not just the unrealized potential of a heterosexual life in America, but also its concomitant repression of the homosexual identity, thus personifying the future consequences of embracing the heterosexual compulsion. That the hero wakes up after the fearful encounter in Alice Staverton's arms suggests a regression to a possibility that had existed before the move to Europe, where the expatriate led, by his own admission, "a selfish frivolous scandalous life" (James JC 2001: 558). Brydon's inability to fully acknowledge or decisively disavow the double means that, irrespective of the reading adopted, he fails to understand the experience as revealing not his potential past self, but the repressed past that is present in the self. Thus, the polarities between the self and the other (in the self), past and present, Europe and America, are problematized, though not entirely dissolved, in this Gothic tale of repatriation.

In another short fiction inspired by James's American tour, "A Round of Visits" (1910), Mark Monteith's encounter with his double takes a different turn, leading to a recognition of the American *alter ego* as part of himself. Monteith's return to New York enacts the disorientation of a man who is only half-present in his travel – he is greatly preoccupied with his personal sorrow and detached from both his surroundings and his past. Monteith comes back to New York after a long absence to assess the loss he has incurred, his small inheritance having been embezzled by a friend,

Phil Bloodgood. It is this "deep sore inward ache" and a bout of grippe that isolate the returnee from other hotel guests, the place itself acting as a figuration of his distress (James RV 1973: 844). Everything around him is experienced as an assault on his senses that makes little sense: the "massive labyrinth" (James RV 1973: 844) of the hotel with its expensive decorations, "the heavy heat, the luxuriance, the extravagance, the quantity, the colour" resembles "some wondrous tropical forest." The hotel guests are likened to "vociferous, bright-eyed and feathered creatures . . . half smothered between undergrowths of velvet and tapestry and ramifications of marble and bronze" (James RV 1973: 847). The whole social scene at the hotel strikes him, moreover, as "the nursery and the playground" (James RV 1973: 846–7), suggesting infantile entertainments and cushioned comfort, reminiscent of the "human felicity" at the Waldorf-Astoria hotel in *The American Scene*. Monteith's preoccupation with his sorrow and the detachment from the surrounding reality is enacted in his movement through the hotel-labyrinth as a disembodied "bruised spirit" hovering above the scene, so startled by "the fauna and flora" that it "drew in and folded its wings" (James RV 1973: 847). What is implicit in his perceptions is a criticism of American commercial culture, the impressions of the hotel-jungle and its birdlike occupants owing their terms and analogies not just to the character's emotional state but also to his aesthetic and moral opposition to the American reality.

Detached and alienated from the surroundings – from "the great gaudy hotel" – Monteith is also disconnected from his past and therefore unable to make sense of his experience (James RV 1973: 844). Robbing him of his money, Bloodgood has gone off "with all the broken bits of the past, the loose ends of old relationships, that he [Monteith] had supposed he might pick again" (James RV 1973: 851). With his hopes thus shattered and only the present pain informing his vision, the movement through New York streets to "pick" one of the "old relationships" mirrors the lack of continuity, and the emptiness of the future as Monteith contemplates "vague crossroads, radiations of roads to nothing" or "the long but still sketchy vista . . . of the northward Avenue, bright and bleak, fresh and hard" (James RV 1973: 851). The alienating hotel with the dehumanized, animal-like guests is now replaced by distorted city images – "a choked trolley-car that howled . . . beneath the weight of its human accretions" and the "suffering shriek of another public vehicle," which render the city unreal and hostile (James RV 1973: 854). While the streets of New York do not evoke memories – they are revived during the first of the eponymous "round of visits." At Mrs. Ash's, who used to live in Europe, Monteith finds the parlour he visited in Paris faithfully recreated and, for the first time since his arrival, remembers the past.

The past evoked during Monteith's next visit allows him to make a connection between the past and the present, furthering his understanding. The visit at Newton Winch's, who has been recently down, like Monteith, with the "grippe" prompts an identification with the other. It is not only the illness that seems to justify the analogy: seeing the previously "coarse" and "common" schoolmate spectacularly improved – Winch seems to have "undergone since their last meeting some extraordinary process of refinement" – Monteith, like Brydon Spencer, wonders if he had perhaps missed this process of change, which would have happened had he stayed in New York (James RV 1973: 856). This conflation of the self and the other makes it possible to regard Winch as representing Monteith's *alter ego* – his unrealized or repressed American self. Because of some features of his appearance Winch is also associated with Phil Bloodgood, which further enhances the mysterious links, relations and associations that arise on the meeting and culminate in the final insight. Eventually, Winch turns out to be, like Bloodgood, an embezzler of other people's money, waiting now for the police to arrest him. The host's subsequent suicide marks a shift in Monteith's perception of himself and reality: when the police officer arriving at the scene asks him if he could not have prevented the accident, he responds that he "must practically have caused it" (James RV 1973: 866). The recognition of his responsibility as one of the people who have lived comfortably in Europe off the proceeds from financial investments in America, thus creating a demand for risky schemes, involves a new consciousness of his participation in the observed reality. Not only is Monteith responsible for what has happened but his American double is regarded as part of himself, it is all involved parties' desire for profit that has driven the financial operations. What this sudden insight also entails is the collapse of the binary oppositions that have so far organized Monteith's perceptions: self and other, victim and perpetrator, Europe and America, suggesting a possibility for a less polarized vision of reality.

In *The American Scene*, "A Round of Visits," and "The Jolly Corner," the nostalgic returns to America take the travellers back in time, promoting a better understanding of the present experience and the self. New York, in particular, becomes the stage for profound insights involving explorations of connections between the past and the present, the personal and the collective, the self and the other. Emblematic of the writer's "reflective nostalgia," the comments about the early twentieth-century America expressed in the travelogue and the short fictions are often marked by harsh criticism of the mercantile culture, the absence of manners and the disregard for the past. However, as has been argued in the essay, insights are not only generated by way of conscious critical reflection; the encounters with the American scene turn into ghostly returns of the past and the emergence of latent, repressed parts of the self. Unmediated by intellectual criticism, those moments evince a conception of experience different from the measure-taking and sense-making engagement with the observed reality. If, as the writer observes in *The American Scene*, "[w]e capture verily, I think, nothing; we merely project," those moments allow the narrator and the characters to respond to experience in a manner that bypasses the (projecting) intellect, replacing the critical engagement with America, that thrives on opposition and conflict, with a recognition of unanticipated relations and connections, which looks ahead to a more self-aware and less polarized future (James *AS* 1994: 243).

Bibliography

Boym, Svetlana (2007) "Nostalgia and Its Discontents," *The Hedgehog Review*, vol. 9, no. 2, Summer: 7–18.

Graham, Wendy (2010) "Social Sciences and the Disciplines," *Henry James in Context*, edited by David McWhirter, Cambridge: Cambridge University Press: 310–20.

James, Henry (1962) Preface to *The Princess Casamassima: The Art of the Novel*, New York: Charles Scribner's Sons: 59–69. Originally published 1908.

—— (1973) "A Round of Visits" *The American Novels and Stories of Henry James*, edited by F. O. Matthiessen, New York: Alfred A. Knopf: 844–66. Originally published 1910.

—— (1986) Preface to *Roderick Hudson: The Art of Criticism*, edited by William Veeder and Susan M. Griffin, Chicago: University of Chicago Press: 3–19.

—— (1994) *The American Scene*, edited by John F. Sears, New York: Penguin Books. Originally published 1907.

—— (2001) "The Jolly Corner," *Selected Tales*, edited by John Lyon, New York: Penguin Books: 550–76. Originally published 1908.

—— (2008) *The Complete Letters of Henry James 1872–1876*, vol. 1, edited by Pierre A. Walker and Greg W. Zacharias, Lincoln and London: University of Nebraska Press.

Rushdie, Salman (1991) *Imaginary Homelands: Essays and Criticism 1981–1991*, London: Granta.

Savoy, Eric (1999a) "The Queer Subject of 'The Jolly Corner.'" *The Henry James Review*, vol. 20, no.1: 1–21.

—— (1999b) "Spectres of Abjection: The Queer Subject of James's 'The Jolly Corner,'" *Spectral Readings: Towards a Gothic Geography*, edited by Glennis Byron and David Putnam, London: Palgrave Macmillan: 161–74.

—— (2010) "Urbanity," *Henry James in Context*, edited by David McWhirter, Cambridge: Cambridge University Press: 354–63.

Index

For Product Safety Concerns and Information please contact our EU
representative GPSR@taylorandfrancis.com
Taylor & Francis Verlag GmbH, Kaufingerstraße 24, 80331 München, Germany

www.ingramcontent.com/pod-product-compliance
Ingram Content Group UK Ltd.
Pitfield, Milton Keynes, MK11 3LW, UK
UKHW021258130625
459435UK00023B/118

* 9 7 8 1 0 3 2 6 5 3 5 3 2 *